ONLY BOUNDERS RIDE M

100 Hundred Years of Family Motorcycling

ONLY BOUNDERS RIDE MOTORCYCLES

100 Hundred Years of Family Motorcycling

*To Bill,
Best Wishes
and Happy Memories*

Ken Mellor

© Ken Mellor, 2016

Published by OK Rollem Productions

email: okrollem@gmail.com
Tel: 01757 617299

A CIP catalogue record for this book is available from the British Library.

ISBN 978-1-5262-0667-1

Book layout and cover design by Clare Brayshaw

Prepared and printed by:

York Publishing Services Ltd
64 Hallfield Road
Layerthorpe
York YO31 7ZQ

Tel: 01904 431213

Website: www.yps-publishing.co.uk

To the memory of Chief Operators.
A once numerous occupation.

Introduction

Before commencing work on the manuscript for the book, I was pondering the idea of writing the whole text in the style of a third person, rather than suddenly appearing in the mid-thirties with constant references to I, me or my. It was also suggested I merely relate the facts to another writer and become the second character at the appropriate event in the story.

That I chose not to adapt the thought will become apparent in the following pages. Having been a part of the story for the last 82 years, will, I hope allow an authentic and personal approach to telling the events I was involved in and being an avid listener and blessed with a good memory, I can vouch with a great deal of accuracy for the events and stories during the eighteen years I missed. To help in telling the story, I have been aided by copious notes that Dad kept in the early 1920s of journeys made and of events, disastrous or otherwise, that occurred during his early motorcycling years.

To help the narrative, once again I am fortunate that Dad had a passion for photography from his early teen years. Helped no doubt by the fact that he followed his father into the fledgling cinema business in Leeds at the age of 13 (he was born in 1901). I am, therefore, able to illustrate the passing years with an abundant selection of photographs.

Any milestone of 100 years is an achievement. To have been a part of it and to have been able to write about it has in itself become very satisfying. With the marker post now falling behind and the future, as always that obscure prospect, all I can now do is place my trust in other powers, with the hope that I may be permitted for some time to come to venture out on 2-wheels and enjoy that stimulation of leaning into a bend, or moving to a higher gear as the engine begins to accelerate. I am the last of this line of Bounders with no one to take over the proverbial baton of membership to a family of motorcyclists that may have been able to take the story further into the 21st century.

To span one hundred years in any subject must inevitably throw down a challenge to make comparisons. In motorcycling the obvious one is mechanical advancement, but other factors must be compared, such as social status. Motorcycles have always been the Cinderella in road transport circles and the bad press notices received by them can only be laid at the feet of motorcyclists. There has developed a love-hate relationship between the rider and the driver where speed above all else is the crucial factor at the expense of those old fashioned values, such as courtesy, road sense, patience and law abiding behaviour. At one time and certainly within my memory, the first motorcycle was often a precursor to better things. By the time a change to four wheels came, road craft and skills were already engrained, plus an understanding of the limitations of two wheels when cocooned in the relative safety of a saloon car.

But the following pages are not written as a social history. It is a story about a father and son and their love of motorcycles. Many of the photographs are from family albums and ownership is duly noted. Copyright holders, where known, are credited to other illustrations and if anyone has been overlooked, I can but apologise and assure them that it was unintentional. I must also acknowledge, yet again the welcome assistance of Eddie Rothwell, whose critical appraisal of my manuscript did much to enhance the final presentation.

1:   The First Twenty Five Years
1916 to 1941

Perhaps I should first explain the origin of the book's title. It comes from no lesser a personage than King George V who delivered his acerbic opinion upon hearing his two sons had taken to riding motorcycles in the grounds of Windsor Castle. It was reputed that the younger Bertie (later to become King George VI), had ridden from Windsor to Sandringham. In the fashionable twenties when young men became trendsetters in the new 'jazz' age, the term was adopted by those motorcyclists adorned with nothing more than blazers and Oxford bags. It became the fashion to ride with your cap turned back to front. You were now a bounder. Reference to the Oxford English Dictionary gives the definition of Bounder as; 'One whose moral conduct is objectionable.' However, an article in Motor Cycling in 1915 waged a campaign to stop riders wearing their peaked caps the wrong way round, adding that superior people regard anyone adopting this style of headgear as a Bounder. As the author of this family history, I am, not unnaturally, biased in favour of the motorcyclist and yet I have a foot in the camp against the wearing of reversed peak caps. Like the man once said, "I think I am indecisive, but I can't make up my mind."

To the ordinary man in the street and from where the mass appeal of motorcycling was to grow in the intervening years prior to world war two, such styles or trends meant little. The motorcycle was to become a means by which many could find respite from the toil and drudgery of the workplace. Assuming of course there was work available.

If Dad ever followed the fashion of a bounder, it was never recalled in later years, so it must be assumed that he was one of those ordinary men who went about their work at a time of great upheaval in Britain. He began his working life three months after the start of world war one. Already the war to end all wars had claimed the lives of many fine young men from villages and towns across the land. The carnage of Mons and the sinking of the Luisitania were already passing into history as he exchanged an ancient pedal cycle for petrol power, a still young and faltering means of propulsion. The machine was a 1908 2hp Minerva an early import from a Belgium manufacturer and was already looking very dated on the streets of Leeds. It had been given the registration number U 153. However, there was one salient point to which he would constantly refer in later years, the fact that it was an all chain drive machine.

The mechanics and mysteries of a motorcycle were to present no problems. Having left school at the age of thirteen, he was already in his second year in the still expanding cinema industry and had become adept at maintaining unreliable film projectors in the confines of a cast iron projection box. Added to this was the ever present danger from nitrate film.

Motorcycling at this period could not have been simpler. You applied for a licence, paid a fee and signed your name in the presence of a town hall clerk and the freedom of the open road was yours. Keeping the machine running was another matter. Information was scant other than what a dealer might pass on, but he was soon to find like-minded fellows who were asking the same questions about mixture settings, ignition timing and belt repair. At least the Minerva had the edge on the latter problem. Manufactures' names were to become as familiar as local street names and would remain in his memory for recall in later years whenever the topic turned to the early days of motorcycling. Bosch, Senspray, Palmer, Pratts and many others were the brand names of the day.

Those who had predicted the war would be over by Christmas, had of course omitted to say which one, so three festive seasons had passed when the third battle of Ypres was being fought in the Flanders mud. On the home front the little Minerva was not only transport to and from work, but it was providing a competitive element in the form of hill climbs.

These were originally instigated by Owen Brooks, a well-known Leeds cinema pioneer who had been issued with the first registration number U 1. His machine had been put together from available parts and was powered by a Vee-twin JAP engine. It also sported a wicker sidecar and he was often to be found on Beeston Hill, a suburb to the south of the town and when he wasn't challenging motorists to a race, he would be giving rides to local children.

The organised hill climbs came about following complaints from local residents and it was suggested that he moved his activities to some of the hills north of Leeds, such as Harewood, Eccup and Arthington. Other cinema owners were already turning to motoring for it was boom time in the cinema industry and how better to show off their new models to fellow entrepreneurs than at such gatherings in the countryside, always within easy distance of a comfortable public house. Life long friendships were formed at these events as staff and owners showed off their prowess on two or four wheels.

Dad entered his first competitive event in the same week that the Government appealed to owners of cars and motorcycles to stop using them for pleasure. They had already announced a doubling of Income Tax for 1916 as the cost of war soared. Although one saving grace was anyone earning less than £130 per year was exempt! The Minerva was made ready with an eagerness that has been found in most young motorcyclists down the years. Tyres, although lacking tread, were inflated to maximum pressure. Grease was applied to all the obvious places and carburettor jets were cleaned along with the spark plug.

The ride out to Eccup Bank was along Otley Road, now listed as A660, but then a hazardous journey. It was badly maintained once the town boundary was passed with long stretches of loose gravel that was treacherous for even an experienced rider. For the newcomer it was a steep learning curve that had to be faced from the outset. Skills could only be learned in the saddle if the journey was to be completed without a fall or hindrance from other road users. The road to Otley was also the natural route to the Dales and was thronged with cycling clubs at weekends.

Also entered for the hill climb and his travelling companion on this day was, Dick Hopkins. He too had followed his father into the cinema business and would remain a close friend for many years. His allegiance to Triumph motorcycles for over thirty years would long be the butt of light banter. He was to be a regular customer at the Leeds depot for Triumph machines and was to become a colleague of the renowned Yorkshire motorcyclist, Eric Langton who was employed as an apprentice mechanic.

An early arrival at the starting point gave time for last minute adjustments, also to sample the fare on offer at the kitchen door of the nearby farmhouse. Each competitor was to be allowed three runs up the hill with the best time being considered for entry on the results sheet.

Although well out in the country, these were public roads with the possibility that a farm cart or a herdsman and his stock might be around the next bend. As a precaution, a simple flag system was in operation to show, as the printed programme quaintly indicated, 'that the coast was clear.' Those in charge of the signals were listed in the programme as 'flaggers' and had been enlisted from Leeds Motor Club.

Despite pushing the rickety Minerva to limits beyond its endurance, it was up against a formidable hill and the townscape of Leeds had not prepared him for this. Although disappointed, he did note that the more powerful machines were all driven by belt.

The return home was uneventful, save for stopping at a roadside hut to purchase petrol dispensed from 2-gallon cans. There were rumours that the price of petrol was to rise to three shillings (15p) a gallon due to the war. This was not good news for a fifteen year old motorcyclist. The popularity of the hill climbs continued despite the restrictions the Government tried to impose so in order to bring a little authority to the somewhat haphazard organisation, the event was brought within a group known as the Leeds Film Exchange. These were heady times in the West Riding for the cinema and film industry with several film producers on the verge of greater things. One of whom was Herbert Wilcox, later to produce and direct a number of classic British films between the thirties and the fifties. He also became the husband of British star, Anna Neagle. At this early period Hollywood was nothing more than a group of orange groves far away in California!

As 1917 dawned, Dad was offered a machine which, as the salesman stated, "Would broaden his horizons." This was a 1914 3½hp Blackburne which looked a huge machine alongside the Minerva. The Leeds registration number was U 3941. Having done a mental calculation, he realised it equated to 496cc and would have an abundance of power. But there were new skills to learn, such as repairing the leather drive belt and the still temperamental gas lighting.

Undaunted, a deal was done, even showing a small profit on the Minerva and he wheeled the Blackburne out of the dealers workshop on the understanding that it would be pushed home. Who among us could resist the temptation, once a corner had been turned, to try out our new purchase and Dad was no exception. There was petrol enough in the tank and two hours to lighting up time, even the road had a favourable down grade as a further invitation. The Blackburne started easily and with a great deal of noise from the tail pipe was soon into its stride.

His immediate impression was how much more power was available and how convenient it was to use the gears neatly built into the rear hub. There was just time to show the new purchase to Dick Hopkins, even though it meant crossing the town with its myriad of trams and treacherous lines. But he blended in with the rest of the lumbering traffic and was able to spend a pleasant hour with his pal before each would commence their evenings work.

His performances in hill climbs did improve but never to the extent of achieving 'fastest time of the day.' He would own the Blackburne for the next eight years during a period of enormous social and economic change following the end of world war one. There was boom and bust along with political and industrial unrest and a work force without work. The return to peace meant different things to many people. By coincidence, The Armistice had been signed on Dad's seventeenth birthday at a time when he was making rapid progress in his work. He was already running a complete show at one cinema, while working as a relief during afternoon matinees at another. The shortage of manpower on the home front had been beneficial to some.

It was decided to mark the return to peacetime motoring with a November hill climb. There were already rumours circulating that the Government was looking to ban pace making and speed events on public roads, so the organisers were expecting a good turn out. Eccup Bank was chosen for the event, a favourite with many competitors. The motorists enjoyed the comfort of the nearby New Inn, while the motorcyclists preferred mugs of tea and beef sandwiches from the farm near the start line. Dad remembered a good time was had by all, although nothing came his way when the awards were announced. The cups and shields were donated by local companies or other members of the Leeds Film Exchange, which, following The Armistice was to be known as the Yorkshire Cinema Trade Exchange. As a lighthearted interlude I can reveal a story Dad often related about the 'goings on' behind the Trade Exchange doors. It was a daily gathering place for cinema owners, film salesmen and representatives from film production renters. Around 3 o'clock most weekday afternoons a ritual was performed, when someone would decide if it was time to go back to work or have another drink. It was decided by them throwing their hats in the air with the promise that if they stayed up they would return to work. If they came down, they would all have another drink!

As 1918 drew to a close, people were looking forward to their first Christmas free from the doom and gloom of daily war reports that had plagued their lives since 1914. The New Year brought more turmoil as the country was beset with strikes by miners, railway workers and dockers. Petrol prices rose to 3 shillings and sixpence a gallon (17 ½p) and unemployment was to reach 2 ¼ million. Amid all the chaos the cinema business was able to provide a screen image of escapism that enabled the public to step out of their depression into a make believe world of action, romance, pathos and comedy. All available within cosy and warm surroundings and often within a short distance from their own cramped and difficult accommodation.

Dad was a purveyor in this near fantasy world, where flickering shadows projected onto a silver screen could evoke tears, laughter or sympathy in little more than an hour. Unbeknown, he had been drawn into a life of entertainment through his father, Charles Mellor. He had begun with a troupe of entertainers around 1907, billing themselves as, The Imperial Pierrots. While still at school, Dad would sometimes appear in a comedy sketch with the 'Imps' that involved throwing custard pies! He also had two uncles on his mother's side who were established in the music halls with their daring high wire act. Then Charles turned his attention to the new cinema fad and began touring the north of England showing films in halls and chapels. Whenever possible, Dad would accompany him, thereby learning the 'nuts and bolts' of the new pleasure medium. Helping to keep the Model T Ford car running smoothly between venues was another edification that would serve him well in the years ahead.

As a new decade began Dad and the Blackburne were venturing further afield. Although lacking paint and nickel plate it was a reliable machine and journeys well over 100 miles were commonplace. Trips to the sea, both east and west coasts were favourable outings with perhaps a preference for Scarborough due to the easier grades. Although Barton Hill just before Malton could be tricky. Now part of the A64 it is a high speed dual carriageway with barely a hint of a gradient, but in 1920, being single track and an uneven surface, it was a stiff test, more so if you were unable to get a good run past Barton le Willows.

On a Sunday in April, 1920 and probably the first visit of the year to the seaside, Dad was in trouble when the drive belt snapped before the top. The Blackburne veered to the roadside, the front wheel running into a drainage channel, which immediately lifted the beaded edge tyre from the rim. His cinema pal, Dick Hopkins, was following on a recently refurbished war department Triumph and being reluctant to lose momentum, was pleased to be given a 'keep going' signal from Dad. They were both trying to make up time to catch up with another work colleague, Joe Buckler. He had recently acquired a Levis 2-stroke, declaring this would be an end to troublesome valves and tappets, but it was no speedster and they usually had to give him five miles start on most long journeys.

Refitting the tyre and repairing the belt were completed but it was going to be hopeless trying to restart on the hill, leaving the only option to return to the bottom and make another attempt, which proved successful. Within the hour the three of them were sitting down to the traditional meal of fish and chips at a regular establishment that boasted the fish had been swimming about less that five hours earlier. In recounting the day out later, Dick Hopkins had declared he knew Joe was up in front because he could smell the 2-stroke exhaust right up to arrival at Scarborough.

It was enough to convince Joe that the Levis did lack that deluxe quality where performance was concerned so he too went along to the Triumph depot and acquired one of the Model H machines that were being renovated for civilian use after war service. The word 'Renovated' actually appeared on the tank, otherwise it was just like a new machine.

Joe and his brother, Frank, were to leave the cinema business and open their own successful engineering company at Morley, Leeds. Between them, they designed and patented a revolutionary pair of nutcrackers guaranteed not to damage the kernel. Dad was presented with one of the first off the production line, which I still have.

It was around this time that Oliver Langton appeared on the scene and even entered some of the hill climbs. He was the elder brother of Eric and we shall meet both of them again in later pages. Oliver had no connection to the cinema business, other than being an ardent patron at several picture houses around south Leeds. Being a Yorkshireman, he was quick to find which ones had a chief operator with a motorcycle enabling him to have a regular supply of complimentary tickets. In their later years, both brothers had fine collections of vintage cars and motorcycles.

Sunday, 27 June 1920 was the first trip of the year to Blackpool. Planned no doubt to take advantage of the long day light hours, thereby saving on the finicky acetylene lighting. But it was going to be a day to remember. The preferred route from Leeds was out along the familiar road to Otley and Ilkley. Then on the Skipton and Clitheroe road to Preston and Blackpool, missing out many of the busy mill towns. In later years, prior to the outbreak of world war two in fact and when I was a trainee sidecar passenger on my mother's knee, there was always great excitement near Blackburn for it was here we would pass the end of the lane with a signpost which led to the village of Mellor. Wonderful tales were told to a wide eyed five year old of the family castle that now stood in ruins and it being how Grandfather came to be known as Charlie Mellor from Mellor! Fifty years later, when I finally found time to drive into the village, how those boyhood illusions were shattered!

But to return to 1920, Dad and Joe Buckler had made an early start, aiming for a lunchtime arrival. The Blackburne had been fitted with a new drive belt, so there was the probability of a roadside stop to remove a link as the new belt settled in. They were also trying to avoid Alan! He was not one of the 'cinema' crowd, in fact his family had a flourishing tailoring factory in the town so he was not without means. This was borne out by the 1919 Scott he had recently purchased. Alan had no interest in clothing manufacture, all he wanted to do was open his own cinema, hence his reason for 'hanging out' with all the motorcycling projectionists. The fact that he finally achieved his ambition does dispel the general opinion at the time that he was just a playboy dreamer. He did, however, lack patience and could not bare stopping for roadside repairs, preferring to ride ahead several miles and wait for others to catch up, then off into the distance he would go again.

By the time they had passed Skipton there had been two roadside halts. The expected belt adjustment by Dad and Joe having to change a sparking plug on his Triumph. Alan had outsmarted himself by taking the wrong road out of Skipton, so had to make top speed to catch up. As he overtook the duo heading towards Clitheroe he gave them a cursory wave before opening the throttle lever and accelerating away despite an approaching corner. He never really saw the farmer frantically waving his arms as he leaned into the bend. The stockman was trying to alert him about some cattle that had strayed onto the road, but it was too late for

Alan who had little chance of making a brake application. A herd of cows on the road are not going to move quickly, even assuming he had time to sound his Klaxon hooter. He became wedged between two cows but the momentum was sufficient to propel him over the handlebars and onto the back of another.

When Dad and Joe pulled into the side there was already a fracas developing as to who was to blame. The farmer was concerned about injuries to his beasts, while Alan was protesting about the damage to his machine and the fact that he could no longer proceed on his journey. Having had a Grammar School education and having developed a cultured voice to match, Alan was now claiming that he had a strong legal case against the farmer for neglecting to maintain fences and allowing cattle to stray onto the King's highway. By now other motorists had stopped and two of three of them were supporting the negligent claim against him. The last thing the farmer wanted was the might of any litigation and realising that he was on the losing side, he condescended to taking the damaged Scott to a garage in nearby Barnoldswick. From that day forth, Alan acquired the nickname, 'Bronco,' not always used to his face though as his sense of humour, along with his pride, were never the same after that day. Dad was also annoyed because, being late arriving in Blackpool, he was unable to call at Fleetwood and buy some freshly smoked kippers for his Mother.

The summer continued with more outings. Wharfedale being a particular favourite. One of the trips took in a hill climb at Park Rash, Kettlewell, though as a spectator on this occasion. It was a formidable climb of loose gravel at a ruling gradient of 1 in 4 and not for the faint hearted. Even with the present tarmac surface it can be a rigorous test of nerve either up or down. At the meeting were some prominent riders of the period. Billy Pratt of Panther Motorcycles and Bertie Jenkins who later became the Triumph dealer in Leeds. Also Jack Carr. Jack was the father of Eric Carr, who was to become a legendary name in Yorkshire grasstrack racing in the 1950s and with who I was destined to have many wheel to wheel battles. It must have been a pleasant return trip home for Dad added a diary page footnote remarking that Wharfedale was looking at its best, also noting that in August a national trial was to include Park Rash as one of the tests hills.

This was the ACU Six Days Trial, an event that had been held since 1903, except for the war years. It had gained a fearsome reputation as the ultimate test for man and motorcycle and as the whole trial was centred on Yorkshire for 1920 there were some of the steepest climbs in the County to be faced. Such names as Sutton Bank, Rosedale Chimney, Holme Moss, Wass Bank and of course Park Rash. Two diary pages are taken up with days spent at Sutton Bank, Wass Bank and Park Rash. This was one advantage of working in the cinema business, except for a mid-week matinee, the working day did not usually start until first house at 6pm. leaving a full day to take in outside events. Always assuming there had been no equipment breakdowns or newly delivered films that required repairing or splicing.

Sutton Bank even in the 21st century can present an arduous challenge for both the apprehensive and the self-assured. Despite such luxuries as 4-wheel drive, automatic transmission, or even synchro-mesh on first gear with a manual gearbox, the danger of being baulked on the approach to one of the tight hairpin bends can be awesome. To jump forward in time to the fifties, I well remember being entertained on a summer Sunday afternoon by the antics of Austin sevens, Morris eights and Ford tens as they attempted the climb. Few cars of this period would have a handbrake capable of holding the vehicle on such a steep gradient. I can even recall some attempts being made in reverse gear as on some cars this was the lowest ratio gear.

But to return to 1920. Dad along with Dick Hopkins and Joe Buckler had made an early start to obtain themselves a good position for viewing, having parked their machines close to the start of the climb. Dad always had a copy of the Michelin Guide with him when out on long journeys and after a stop in Thirsk for morning tea, the Guide advised them that 'Sutton Bank at a gradient of one in three and a half was only possible for very powerful cars.' On their walk towards the summit they passed a local breakdown lorry which was recovering a 25hp Vauxhall, on this occasion coming down having failed to brake for the bend. The mechanic informed them that it was his third job that morning and it was still only 10am.

A good vantage point was the first bend, giving a view of the approach and the continued climb (hopefully) towards the next bend. No programme was available, but several marshalls were in attendance who were able to pass on such information as expected times and who to look out for as the most likely to make successful climbs. They did not have too long to wait either, for the sound of a 2-stroke machine could be heard being mercilessly flogged to the limit of it's power. In to view came the rider and machine accompanied by cheers and applause from the spectators, especially from Joe, as the machine was a Levis ridden by Gus Kuhn. He made it to the first bend and sent several marshalls scattering when he took the outside of the bend to reduce the inside steep gradient. By using both legs for propulsion and balance, he was round and off towards the top of the hill, leaving onlookers gasping in amazement. Especially, Joe Buckler, who's own experience of riding a Levis 2-stroke was certainly a lot less impressive than what they had just seen.

From then on there was a steady stream of riders, some successful, others entertaining to the gathering and some who had to throw in the towel before reaching the first bend. But it was two hours of heroic exploits on 2-wheels. Wass Bank was six miles away and they could spend about an hour before setting off back to Leeds and an evenings work. Again it was the performances of the Levis machines that made an impact on all of them, especially when they discovered one of the team riders was F.W.Applebee, or 'Pa' as he was known by. Not without good reason too, for he had ridden in the first T.T. Races in 1907 at the age of 46 and had only two months earlier finished third in the Lightweight T.T. Riding a Levis.

Wass Bank is approached from Coxwold, a delightful village on the fringe of the Howardian Hills and probably little changed from when the ACU Six Days Trial centred on it in 1920. The climb looks straight forward enough with no severe bends, but it can be deceiving as the surrounding landscape gives an impression that the gradient is easing at a point where more power is needed. Many of the competitors had stopped near the scenic ruins of Byland Abbey before attempting the climb and our trio were able to see many of the 'big' names who were leading the field at this early stage, including of course the Levis team who, with Joe's enthusiasm, had become the centre of their attention. 'Pa' Applebee, who, at 59 was older than all their fathers by at least eight years.

They listened in awe as 'Pa' was telling someone the story of how, in the 1909 T.T. He had to throw a jug of cold water over his cylinder at the bottom of Glen Helen Hill every lap to enable him to climb the hill.

Two days later they were back at the now familiar Park Rash climb at Kettlewell and again they were amongst names that they had only read about in the motorcycling press. Jack Marshall and Frank Hulbert riding for Triumph, Len Crisp on a Humber and closer to home, Matt Rowley, Harry Langman and Harry Shackleton all mounted on Scotts. Dad always claimed there was nothing to compare with the sound of a Scott, either climbing Park Rash or flat out past the grandstand at Douglas, Isle of Man. But rumours were circulating that some of the leaders had come to grief on Rosedale Chimney, so the field could be depleted.

The ride back to Leeds was not without some drama. After passing through Otley and just before beginning the long climb of Otley Chevin, the Blackburne picked up a nail in the rear tyre. Having already been delayed with a broken mudguard stay and time running short before starting work, some ingenuity was called for. They were next to a field that had just been harvested so there was a plentiful supply of hay. The beaded edge tyre was already off the rim and in no time it was stuffed with best quality Yorkshire rye. "Never stick fast," was a well used saying in our house, although Dad would sometimes use a more cultured version, "Needs must when the devil drives." I confess to having used both versions most of my adult life. Punctures were the downside of motorcycling during the early part of the twentieth century, nails of the horse shoe variety being a common cause. But the condition of the roads could be another reason, not helped by the vulnerable fitting of beaded edged tyres. Dick Hopkins once encountered another puncture hazard when he was following a Foden steam lorry through Leeds. The lorry had just crossed a tramway junction with some very uneven cobble stone setts causing hot coals to fall from the ashpan. Having very little tread on the front tyre was not a help either as he tried to steer the rapidly deflating tyre and wobbly Triumph to the kerb side.

Vibration was also a problem which was compounded by rigid frames, minimal fork springing and road surfaces with a condition that would not be tolerated in our 'new age' culture of seeking justice by litigation. Late in the summer of 1920 the usual crowd were planning a trip to Scarborough. Joe's brother, Frank, had just purchased a 1914 Rudge with the popular multi gear. Rudge had recently opened their depot in Leeds and it was already becoming the place to meet for the 'in crowd.' One of the machines on display was G.G. Pullin's machine which had won the

1914 Senior T.T. The last before world war one began and it was in fact 1920 before racing resumed on the Island.

Frank's bike was the centre of attention and he was building up the T. T. performance perhaps more than was justified. Whether or not Dad mentioned to him that Blackburne machines had finished second and third in the Junior T.T. three months earlier is not recorded. They were some miles past York, when Dick Hopkins had to make a stop to adjust the drive belt. It was while parked in a gateway that someone noticed petrol dripping from a tank seam on the Rudge and fuel was running down towards the silencer box. They were probably beyond the point of no return, so it was down to the inventiveness of young minds to find a solution. If a can could be wedge in a position to catch the drips, some distance could be covered before returning the fuel to the tank. A nearby repair garage had a yard full of old containers and a suitable size was found. A mechanic even cut off the top to make a larger aperture and they were soon off again. They had to stop about every four or five miles to decant fuel back to the tank, but they made it to the sea front.

As they prepared for the return journey, Frank felt he could not face the 65 mile trip and decided to put the Rudge on a Leeds bound train, where, his brother Joe would meet him and ensure a safe arrival home. The sun was still high as they headed west and it was an easy journey to Malton, but there was a likely chance of a hold up at the level crossing. Rail traffic was much more frequent then resulting in several dozens of cars waiting. Forty years into the future the numbers would be counted in hundreds. In the 1950s, Dad and I devised our own bypass to the south of the town. It was longer but a much quieter route and therefore more satisfying. Had we waited another thirty years, the 4 mile bypass solved the whole problem. But by then the level crossing was no longer troublesome. Doctor Beeching had made sure of that.

The diary entries for the rest of 1920 make no mention of further trips to the coast but there is an interesting entry for August 30 which highlights the achievement of a 31 year old railway guard who won gold medals for Britain in the 800 metres and 1500 metres at the Olympic Games held in Antwerp. With no more seaside outings and living close to his workplace, the Blackburne was laid up for general maintenance but several times had to be called upon in an emergency to recover a film programme. At this period all films were delivered by rail and it could be very unreliable to say the least. It was not unknown for them to be dropped off at a station several miles away, which is what happened on this occasion when the porter at Wakefield took out the wrong wicker basket that held the reels of film and left it on the platform for collection. This was how Dad found it with several feet of Mary Pickford's new release trailing on the rain soaked platform. It happened to be reel one and when it was shown for the first time, the manager came up to the operating box and said,

"I don't like these new opening effects that Hollywood are using." The name of the film was 'Suds.'

1921 started with grim news about unemployment. It was to rise to over 2 million, but so too were womens skirts which prompted one newspaper to print the banner headline, 'Skirts have been steadily rising since the war! But there was good news for those without work, the unemployment benefit was to rise to 18 shillings a week. By the time spring arrived and the 'gang' of four were ready for the road, there had been some change of mounts. Frank Buckler had bought himself a 1920 Scott, while brother Joe had placed an order for the recently announced Triumph Ricardo. This left Dad with a very out dated looking motorcycle, although vintage was not yet the appropriate word to use and there were still many other fully belt drive machines in use. One of these belonged to Dad's assistant operator, Herbert, and it was his first motorcycle so he was looking for tuition. This was a 1919 350cc Rex fitted with a Blackburne engine.

As they were both keen swimmers and they had a spare day until 6pm, it was decided to head for the coast to enjoy the sea off Filey. At this period there was no weather forecasting, nor was there any radio, save for the crackling reception of a crystal set and headphones, so other than what a fir cone may indicate and looking to the sky for clouds on the horizon, it was down to the vagaries of the English weather. As they headed east they were aided by a breeze at their backs, which as any motorcyclist will agree is a rare event. It all made for a good run and Herbert had coped well on his first long distance outing. Being able to park their machines on the beach meant they were soon in the water and with a convenient diving platform moored just offshore which, being out of season, they had to themselves.

More than an hour had passed when they realised that the tide was ebbing and there was a stiff breeze from the west. Swimming back to the beach became an all-out effort, which in later years Dad would recall with some uneasiness and I don't think he swam in the sea again. By the time they were mobile, it was clear that they would have a head wind all the way and with around sixty miles to cover and just three hours before patrons would be queueing for tickets, there was concern that as the show could not start before they arrived, there would be some explaining to be done. As they joined the main road to York they were straight into the west wind, although the gradients were in their favour. Dad had already advised Herbert to try and stay directly behind him, although any effect of slip streaming was minimal. What they really needed was a large and slow moving van, preferably going all the way to Leeds, to provide some respite from the buffeting.

They were in luck. Within three or four miles they caught up with a suitable vehicle. This was a large box type van and as it had a sign giving a York address, they kept behind. It was not entirely a fool proof plan, for upon arriving in Malton the driver turned into a factory yard to make a delivery. But the last ten miles had been bearable. Dad was now worried that York with it's narrow streets would cause more time to be lost, so it meant struggling on, despite Herbert looking somewhat pale. If he was to become a motorcyclist this was some initiation test. I have lost count of the number of times I heard this story recalled and by the time I was in my teens, I could recount it with Dad word for word, how he shouted out with joy when the Leeds boundary sign appeared, how he had already compiled a story to tell the manager and the dismay on arrival of seeing the queue of customers waiting in the side street which he immediately took to be due to his late arrival. Leaning the Blackburne against the wall and instructing Herbert to wheel both machines into the cinema yard, he dashed to the entrance only to find it deserted. It was then that the cashier told him about the manager having to return home to collect the keys for his office, along with the cash float for the pay boxes. For the rest of his life he would always insist in having double the time when preparing for any journey, be it by bus,train, car or motorcycle!

The Blackburne had performed heroic deeds that day. Being held at almost full throttle for mile after mile yet achieving a road speed that could only be described as mediocre in the battle with the westerly wind, had caused the engine to overheat. Dad claimed he remembered looking down and seeing the first six inches of the exhaust pipe glowing a dull red. In my first years of motorcycling and still a novice in the ways of an internal combustion engine, I had always treated this as an exaggeration. That is until I had moved on to my first BSA M20, when after my first attempt at an engine overhaul,including timing the magneto fully retarded, I took the machine out for an evening test run. Although I never mentioned it to him. He was right!

As 1921 moved from spring to summer the Blackburne provided the link that was to lead Dad to a life long partnership. He had become friendly with a girl who worked in one of the pay boxes. No more than pleasantries were exchanged until one night, due to industrial action, the whole of the town's tram network ceased running. Young Grace Gallagher was in a dilemma. She lived a distance to the east of the town and faced a very long walk late at night through gas lit streets. A journey she was not looking forward to. The thought of riding on the rear of a motorcycle not only didn't seem ladylike, but appeared to be fraught with danger, if only from the noise she had heard it make. The suggestion of being thrown from it only came later when her father admonished her for such a foolhardy action. Grace had never even ridden a pedal cycle, nor would she for the rest of her life.

To make the journey easier and to try and add a degree of comfort, a cushion was borrowed from the cinema and placed on the rear carrier. Still doubtful of the correct propriety, she decided to adopt a sidesaddle position for this first experience of 2-wheeled transport. She would remember the 17th May for the rest of her life. Not from exhilaration or elation, but from sheer fright. Picture the scene at 10.30pm. Cobbled streets with dismal gas lighting, tram lines, an adequate though somewhat dated motorcycle with acetylene lamps, belt drive and a girl riding side saddle! Those were the pioneer days.

As weeks passed she began to notice there were many girls riding as a motorcycle passenger, and most of them appeared to be adopting the conventional pillion style. Come the New Year and springtime, in daylight at least she found it quite pleasant and became a regular pillion rider. Although for the sake of family bliss, she always alighted at least two streets away from her home. Her father was still of the belief that motorcycles were a damnation upon mankind!

For this young couple the early twenties were their years. Being born in the first year of the new century they were to experience each changing mode with an acceptance that only young people can tolerate. The period of boom and bust meant little when almost every day brought out new words, new music, daring fashions and a quaint and crackly new entertainment called 'the wireless.' Added to this were the heroes and heroines that smiled or sobbed from flickering screens all over Britain. Going to the pictures would become a natural and respectful event and for young couples it was an approved place for young love to blossom.

For Dad and Mum it was not to be a whirlwind romance. Both parents considered certain conventions must be followed and the practicalities of starting a new life must be carefully considered. A suitable time had to elapse before an engagement could be announced. Even then four years were to pass before they were married. Nevertheless, they celebrated with a trip to Scarborough, by train, and had a studio portrait photograph taken.

1922 was to be an eventful year not only for affairs of the heart. Grandfather Mellor had seen the potential for filming local newsworthy events, not only for sale to the established newsreel companies, but for publicity purposes at cinemas around the town. Another popular sideline was to film the queues that formed outside each cinema before the doors opened with a promise that their friends could see them on the screen next day. To carry the bulky 35mm camera and tripod, Dad bought his first and only car. Naturally it was second hand. In fact it had obviously been through many hands and was to cause some derision not only with friends, but within the family at it's performance, or lack of!

The model was a 1908 Clement-Talbot and it was the 175th car to be registered in Leeds. The first example of it's outmoded appearance came when he proudly offered to take his mother for a tour of the local streets. All was going well and Grandma Mellor was no doubt pleased with her son's new found status, until they came to stop at a road junction, when several street urchins came up and called out, "Cor! Look at this old crock, it's even got doors." She never travelled in it again! An example of the car's velocity happened when Dad and couple of his pals were off for a day out. As is often the way with younger brothers, Leslie also wanted to come along and in order to deter him, he was sent back to fetch his jacket. As soon as he disappeared into the house, Dad put his foot down. Fifty yards up the road, Uncle Leslie caught up with them and jumped into the rear seat!

An even zanier example and one that displays the acumen of 'man's best friend' happened one Sunday. Dad had an affection for Alsatian dogs which had become popular in Britain after world war one. 'Que', or to give him his full Kennel Club name, 'Champion Queno von Brunanoff' had developed a liking for riding in the back seat and would be there whenever he heard the starting handle being turned. On this day Dad wanted to be off without him and shut him in the house. 'Que' had other ideas and went upstairs, nosed up the sash window in one of the bedrooms, leapt into the garden and was soon running alongside.

For the past two or three years there had been constant rumours that the Government were to end sporting motor events on public roads, now it was to become a reality with Legislation before Parliament. Around Britain clubs were preparing for events to mark the passing of this once freedom of our roads for pace making, sprinting and hill climbs. In Leeds, the Yorkshire Cinema and Trade Exchange were planning one last picnic and hill climb for 18th June,1922 at the popular Eccup Bank and invitations were being sent out across the whole of Yorkshire, Cheshire and Lancashire.

On the day there were 36 programme entries plus some late comers, twelve of which were motorcycles, including those who we have already met, namely, Joe and Frank Buckler, Dick Hopkins and Dad. As spring seemed to be in the air when a young man's fancy turns to love, their young ladies were also attending as spectators and before the decade was over, they had all become married. The sun shone, the men tinkered and prepared their machines, while the girls chatted and prepared the sandwiches. Despite no awards being won it was a day they would remember for many years after. Everyone present had come through the last war, the one that was to end all wars! So how could they have possibly imagined that seventeen years hence, they would be drawn into yet another conflict.

For the return journey, Dad decided on an alternative route through pleasant countryside to the north of Leeds. It was truly rural with wooded lanes, fields and working farms and as the Blackburne hummed along with a rhythmic click from the belt coupling link, how could he have possibly imagined he was passing within a mile of where, in 12 years hence, he would be purchasing his first house and raising his second son who would also grow up to be a motorcyclist. But we are getting ahead of the story for there were still difficult years ahead. Unemployment, inflation and industrial unrest were still rampant and economy was now the watchword at this troubled period as employers looked to make savings by reducing wages not only on the factory floor, but in the cinema operating box.

Strange though it may seem, throughout this stringent period cinemas were still opening. Often they were primitive church halls or struggling theatres which were quickly and easily converted for their change of use as more and more people were going to the 'pictures.' Trying to escape from drudgery, cramped living conditions and a frugal life style could be obtained very cheaply. Or as one writer aptly summed up, "They were buying an acre of seats in a garden of dreams." In an attempt to keep up with falling income, Dad moved to a new cinema that was planned to open on Good Friday, 1923. It was across the town, but nearer to where Grace lived and of course he now had a choice of 2-wheels or 4-wheels. There were other advantages too. He was able to ingratiate himself with his future in-laws by a regular offering of complimentary tickets.

Joining him as assistant operator was, Herbert, who by now had become a competent rider on his Rex/Blackburne. He was even more skilled at money making ideas, such as saving old tram tickets when going to the railway station to collect the new film programme and claiming double the expense. The owner of the cinema was a Russian Jewish immigrant with a limited command of English which could only be delivered through a thick East Slavonic accent. He claimed to have avoided capture from his enemies by riding many miles on the back of a Peugeot motorcycle, which may have been the reason why he allowed both machines to be parked under cover in the yard at the side of the cinema. One family story about him that was frequently recounted down the years put a different slant on his sentiment for 2-wheeled transport.

During the silent days of a film programme the speed of the projector could be varied. It was often necessary when the orchestra or pianist and, sometimes a singer had to match the scenes on the screen. On this occasion the singer had to fit his song to the dramatic climax of the film, which meant having to slow down the running speed of the film. As Herbert faded in the final reel he forgot to change the speed notch with the result that the film ended while the singer was one third of the way through his song. Realising they were in trouble, Dad flashed on the 'God

Save the King' slide, switched off the A.C. Generator and both dashed downstairs and were out before the audience.

Next morning the 'boss' came to the operating box and remonstrated them in his best English with, "Vair wos yu last night. Wen I cum to see wat was up, yu all escapading on yer dam blast motibikes. If I had a gun I vud have shot yer." With such a vocabulary life was never dull at the Princess Cinema. In later years when he had prospered and opened a second cinema he became a well-known figure around the local streets as he lauded it up sitting in a BSA sports sidecar. The very same one that I was to begin my motorcycle apprenticeship as a babe in arms.

There were plenty of opportunities for mid-week outings too. On days when there were no film or equipment repairs to be completed, Dad and Herbert, being situated close to the York road, would get away around midday and tour the Yorkshire Wolds, often calling at farms where there was always an abundance of eggs and fruit for sale very cheap. One occasion when they had stopped at a small holding, the owner had found he had a glut of tomatoes and being unable to find a buyer at his wholesale outlet, invited them to help themselves. As Herbert had panniers on his machine he filled them to the brim, but was in for a shock when they arrived back at the cinema. Both panniers were literally dripping tomato puree.

Roadside camaraderie for motorcyclists goes back to the very earliest days of the old century, when seeing a rider crouched alongside his machine would bring the enquiry, "Are you alright?" as you pulled alongside. It may not be as prevalent today with the mobile phone and breakdown or get you home service included in most insurance policies, so as Dad often related, if you offered help, you may be taking on more than you expected. One example occurred when he and Herbert encountered a callow youth on the road to Driffield. He had already been busy with a screwdriver by removing the timing cover and two gearwheels, one of which was already devoid of teeth and the obvious cause of the stoppage. After trying to explain the simple working of the engine and that he would need to buy a replacement gear, the lad wheeled the bike to the edge of the bank and let it slither and slide into a pond and walked off over the field. Dad always remembered the make of machine was Ivy, adding it was also the name of one of the cleaners at the cinema and she was unreliable too!

Another occasion of playing the good samaritan, this time with Dick Hopkins, happened when they were flagged down by a stranded motorist. A child in the car had been stung by a wasp and the mother was distraught because the face swelling was effecting the child's breathing. They had stopped due to a puncture and now needed to find medical attention urgently. The first problem was the mother had never ridden on the back of a motorcycle before, but was prepared to if the child could be accommodated. Dick's Triumph was the more practical machine, so with a blanket added between the saddle and the pillion and the child between them, off they started in the direction of York and medical aid. It was two hours before they returned. The child now calm and the mother quite flushed and exhilarated by her first venture on a motorcycle. For many years afterwards, both Dad and Dick received a Christmas card from the grateful parents.

One story that was frequently told down the years whenever the pals met, even into retirement years concerned a bull. Dad, Dick and Joe Buckler were on their way to Filey, when they came upon a stranded motorcyclist. His problem was the frame of his Norton and broken just below the steering head which allowed the engine to slump almost down to the road surface. Out in the country there is little in the way of mechanical survival, unless you happen to be near a farm or cottage, which on this occasion was not the case. Other than themselves the only other movement was cattle in an adjacent field and Joe surmised they may have a chain or some form of halter around their necks so it was worth investigating. As they went into the field, the cattle began to move away as is their habit. All except for one which appeared to be tethered to a post by a chain, the sort that would serve their purpose ideally. It was Dick who was first to utter a biblical name, then details of the beast's anatomy. As for the bull it was going nowhere and it's attention was firmly fixed on them. The chain was a solid link type which would be perfect for making a temporary repair to the Norton's frame, obtaining it was another matter.

The chain was wrapped around the post with several turns, so that end should not be too much of a problem, unless you count the probability of trying to hold the bull once it was free of the post. Another problem was, assuming they got the chain unconnected at the other end, what were the chances of the bull running away? If the snorting sounds that were becoming louder were a guide, they would be the subject of it's fury. The Norton rider thought they could distract the bull if they put some food down and providing they could cut the rope around it's neck which held the chain, there was a chance of success. They all carried penknives so if there was to be any cutting of the rope Joe thought his would be the sharpest, although he was already thinking of taping it to a long stick or branch to gain some distance between the bull and whoever was going to try.

The next job was to find some food which proved easier than they imagined. Dick Hopkins found some only two or three fields away and came back with a good supply of what looked like Kale or Turnips. The general feeling was that if all four of them were there in the field, causing a diversion in the event of trouble, they could outrun the bull and reach the safety of the fence. So the food was thrown down in front of and all around the bull, the thinking being that it would be confused with choice. And they were right. Joe approached from behind with a well chosen sapling bearing his knife and where the rope passed over the back of the animal, he was able to make rapid cuts. In no more than two or three minutes the rope was cut and the chain fell to the ground making a noise that went unnoticed by the bull. Then it suddenly realised that it was no longer tethered and must have thought all it's birthdays had come at once. As much food as it could eat and at least twenty cows to choose from! The gang had all the time they wanted to remove the chain from the post and soon effected a substantial repair by, first propping up the engine, then wrapping the chain over the frame top tube and back around the engine plates, two or three times. The Norton rider had a pocketful of nuts and bolts, so by passing a few through the chain links it became a very sturdy job. The grateful rider was soon on his way, having noted their addresses with an assurance that he would keep in touch. The fact that he never did had no bearing on the tale. Our heroes had a story that would out last them. Whichever one of them told it, would always begin with the line that, "One year there was a very sudden increase of calves born on a farm out Driffield way."

As summer, 1924, came along there was an announcement of an engagement between Dad and Grace. It seemed a respectful time had passed and they were now thinking of a wedding date in June, 1926. They were good times for many, despite economic difficulties and the forecast of a general strike, even for Dad, it seemed that everything was going well. Then along came 'Nellie!' This was a situation that happened at the cinema and though he always tried to make light of it and often repeated the story, it annoyed him for a good many years. All films produced at this period contained nitrate which made the material highly inflammable. There had been a number of serious fires in cinemas and it had become a requirement of obtaining a licence for the exhibition of films to employ a full time fireman. There were regular inspections by fire departments, covering fire extinguishers and equipment and the handling of and storage of films in the projection box. These visits were not announced and could happen at random on any day and at any time. On this particular day is was a police inspector, not a fireman, who entered the operating box and made straight for the rewind room. Herbert had just come out to check with Dad the running order of the matinee programme leaving the inspector to find an unattended film on the rewind machine. He immediately called for the owner to be present and advised them that, in view of the serious offence he was obliged to issue a summons notice in view of the flouting of fire regulations. He cited Dad, as Chief Operator, that it was his responsibility, also listing Herbert as a conspirator in the offence. The film was a new release by one of the leading stars at the time, Claire Windsor, the title being. 'Nellie, the Beautiful Cloak Model.'

The cinema owner was most anxious to keep the story out of the local paper, going as far as telephoning the editor, but to no avail. When the late edition of the paper arrived, they were shocked by almost banner headlines, 'Nellie on the Bench.' It then gave an account of the misdeed and the neglected reel of film. Dad was fined £2, which was at the time nearly half a weeks income, while Herbert was fined ten shillings. At least the owner had the decency to pay the fines. Nor did he object to the extra takings from full attendances the publicity brought. As for Dad, there was a lighter side to it. Many of his pals now referred to his machine as 'Nellie, 'the Blackburne Model.'

Now that Dad and Grace were, to use that lovely old term, 'walking out together,' she had become interested in Grandfather Mellor's theatrical outlets. In addition to his film rental business, he was also a partner in a theatrical agency and as she had a delightful singing voice, he thought he could find her work in musical chorus productions. She did appear at a number of theatres around the north of England but was unable to adapt to a life of suitcases, catching late night trains and worst of all, theatrical 'digs.'

For 1925 road users had to be come accustomed to Parliament's new legislation in an effort to reduce road accidents. This was a recommendation by the Ministry of Transport to introduce white lines separating traffic streams at intersections and on dangerous bends. Some of the cities and large towns in the North of England were quick to react, but it took much longer for country roads to adopt the scheme.

Joe Buckler had now attached a sidecar to his Triumph Ricardo and brother Frank was also contemplating the idea of building a sidecar to his own specification. It all meant that on trips to the coast more paraphernalia could be taken in the form of Primus stoves, folding seats and their own food. Sporting events were always a favourite with our gang of four and as one of the motorcycle magazines had mentioned a sand racing event at Filey in May to which a number of top name riders had been invited, this sounded an ideal day out. Amongst the names in the programme were Freddie Dixon, George Tottey, Jack Carr and a nineteen year old Oliver Langton, who was becoming well known in Yorkshire speed events. It may be anticipating the story by some twenty four years, but this was the man who would be instrumental in my motorcycle racing future.

It was a simple circuit consisting of two half-mile straights with rounded bends which gave an ample run off area. From the start of practice when they sampled the sound of open exhausts and savoured the fumes of the alcohol fuel intermingled with the aroma of Castrol R they were hooked. Freddie Dixon and George Patchett had given some wonderful displays of flat out riding, along with cornering that left them overwhelmed. From then on they began to follow the exploits of the top road racing men such as, Alec Bennett, Wal Handley, Jimmy Simpson and Stanley Woods but the chances of seeing them in action around the Yorkshire area were nil. Their only hope was a trip to the Isle of Man for the T.T. Races. It had been a memorable day rounded off by a picnic on the beach and the only delay in the journey home was a puncture in the front wheel of Frank's Scott.Before 1925 was out, Frank was to marry, followed in 1926 by brother Joe and Elsie, along with Dad and Grace who I should from now on rightly refer to as Mum! Dick Hopkins and Olive were to wait another two years before tying the knot.

With a wedding planned for June there were all the usual preparations for both families to arrange, although in later years Dad was often heard to sing the middle chorus of the popular song, 'Daisy Daisy', relating "it wouldn't be a stylish marriage, he couldn't afford a carriage." With regard to plans for a honeymoon, both families were surprised by the announcement that it would involve a sea voyage. The Gallagher's naturally assumed it would be to Ireland from where James Gallagher had emigrated to Leeds in 1895, so were somewhat down hearted when they were told it would be to Douglas in the Isle of Man to see the T.T. Races. Such was the couple's enthusiasm they both had a most thrilling week, so much so that they booked for the following year. I believe the racing was exciting too!

Seeing such an array of machines every day they left the hotel, gave Dad a feeling that 'Nellie the Blackburne Model' really was of another age. It was now all chain transmission on every machine that passed by and before they had set sail for home, he had made up his mind that for next year there would not only be a change of machine, he would bring it to the Island. One other highlight of the week, Mum's hero, Stanley woods, won the Senior T.T. riding a Norton.

After their week of initiation to the world of road racing it was back home to begin married life. They had already found rooms at Lofthouse Hall between Leeds and Wakefield. It was somewhat dilapidated and already destined for demolition, but being situated in twenty acres of parkland looked idyllic when the sun was shining. Mum likened it to Bleak House in the Dickens novel and when she was alone at night while Dad was working at the cinema, it was only having the company of Champion Queno von Brunanhoff that she felt secure.

For Dad it was a longer journey to and from work, including climbing Lofthouse Hill on the way home. This was the scene of another incident that would rankle with him for many years after. He was leaving the cinema around 11pm when he noticed the carbide container on the front lamp was low but felt there was enough to provide illumination for the 5 mile journey. He had just reached the top of Lofthouse Hill and only half a mile from the Hall, when he was signalled to stop by a police constable. The front lamp was barely giving a glimmer, although the rear light was still showing an indication of red. Nevertheless, the constable said he would have to issue notice of a summons, despite protests from Dad that he had only three hundreds yards to travel. But to no avail. Then he tried by saying he had only been married for three weeks, but the PC was adamant, the Law had to be obeyed.

The summons duly arrived requiring him to appear at Wakefield Court a week later. The legal description of the offence is worth quoting, if only to illustrate the ornate language that still persisted as legal jargon and little altered from the age of horse drawn vehicles. It began, ' During the period of one hour after sunset and one hour before sunrise, did unlawfully ride a carriage, to wit a motor bicycle, on a highway thereby required to carry an attached lamp so constructed and placed to exhibit a light in the direction in which you were proceeding and kept lighted as to afford adequate means of signalling the approach or position of the said carriage.'

In court he tried to offer the same mitigating circumstances that he had told the constable, but there was no sympathetic ear on the bench and he was fined ten shillings. As he left the court his mind was made up. He would go and put his name on the list to apply for one of the new council houses being built on the edge of the City. At least It would be close to his workplace and his in-laws. To his delight, and Mum's, the application was accepted, with the proviso that without children it would mean a twelve month wait. He just had to ensure that he carried a spare tin of carbide from then on and Mum would have to endure the draughts, rattling windows and lack of hot water for a little longer.

Being summertime meant every opportunity was taken to visit the sea. There now seemed to be a preference for the east coast and certainly for Joe and Frank and their wives, it became more and more their wish to one day retire there. Even Dick Hopkins bought a caravan on a site near Filey just before the outbreak of world war two. Despite the difficult economic times the ten or so years leading up to the war must have been happy and satisfying times for all of them. The notes in Dad's diaries certainly give that impression and some of the reports of breakdowns always give a hint of humour.

One summer weekend Joe Buckler had gone ahead to an almost unknown beach to the south of Bridlington. This had become a particular favourite with all of them, if only for the privacy it offered. Joe was carrying the camping stove, chairs and most of the food which kept his speed to a moderate pace. As he entered a village near to the coast, the sidecar wheel struck a pothole and sheared the stub axle holding the wheel, grounding the chassis and rousing his wife, Elsie, from her knitting. The wheel had damaged the sidecar mudguard but little else, although a roadside repair looked doubtful. Joe walked into the village and found a local blacksmith cum handyman who brought out a flat trolley normally used for carrying milk churns and they returned to the stranded outfit. With the trolley under the chassis it was an easy task to wheel the machine back to the workshop. The wheel had been running on a simple cup and cone bearing which had now disintegrated and lost all the ball bearings. Without portable welding equipment no easy solution could be seen. Then the odd job man suggested a block of wood could be clamped to the chassis, a hole drilled (or burned) to take a spindle and a small wheel fitted. The sort of wheel he had in mind was the type fitted to wheel barrows and as he had one available, Joe decided to take a chance, even if it only lasted to the beach a few miles away.

A solid block was soon mounted, the hole having already been drilled to the required size. In no more than an hour, the outfit was again on all three wheels and a slow test ride along the village street gave every indication of a first class 'Bodge'. For safety's sake, Elsie rode on the pillion for the remaining few miles, even so they were still there before the rest. With everything laid out on the beach no one noticed anything amiss with Joe's machine until the time came for them to head for home. Then he had to come clean and show them the 'make do and mend' fitting. As Elsie was not keen in riding all the way back to Leeds with what she imagined was a wobbly wheel, she opted to ride on the back of Frank's Scott. Joe led the way and so set the speed for the others. As each mile went by he grew more confident with the small barrow size wheel, so much so, that with his engineering prowess he was to modify the crude adaptation into a very credible conversion and in so doing, he was to pre-empt the commercial sidecar manufacturers by around thirty years!

Nellie, the Blackburne model was still running well which showed much credit to the engine design and ruggedness. The makers were in a small way, rivals to the other proprietary engine manufacturer, J. A. Prestwich or JAP as they were more commonly known by. Blackburne's prestige was riding high at the moment, for their engines had taken the first three places in the 1926 Lightweight T.T. Race. However, Nellie came to grief towards the end of the year in a spectacular way while pulling up a modest gradient. The cast iron piston broke up into three or four pieces which in turn caused the cylinder wall to burst open and spill out the contents onto the road. This was one breakdown that had no easy solution and yet in a strange twist of fate, there was to be a satisfactory outcome.

Dad was not far from a cinema that was run by a true veteran of the Leeds cinema scene. Albert Groves had started just before the turn of the old century working as a projectionist with one of several travelling bioscope shows. The travelling showmen visited fairs in the period 1890 – 1914 and were pioneers in the world of cinematograph entertainment advertising each performance with the sounds of a magnificent Gavioli or Marenghi fairground organ, then announcing that the 'moving pictures' were about to start.

Albert listened to Dad's tale of woe, then said he knew someone who had a newish motorcycle for sale following the tragic death of his son. Not as a result of the machine but by some sudden unexpected illness. He promised to let him have further information and in the meantime he could leave Nellie at the back of the cinema. A few days later Albert called to see Dad with details. The machine was a 1925 350cc AJS and the father of the late owner was asking £22, which was around half the purchase price. He had a telephone number but no more details other than an address between Harrogate and Ripon.

Dad made contact with the seller and arranged to call at the weekend. The price amounted to a month's wages so there would have to be some belt tightening. The Blackburne had little value, even if it had been in running order. The Clement-Talbot had now developed a very expensive noise in the engine and was only fit for a trip to Autorex, a well known vehicle breaker in the town and a name in common use amongst car owners when they wanted to be uncomplimentary. It was Albert Groves to the rescue with an offer of a £10 loan. In addition to running his cinema, Albert also dealt in secondhand projectors so a deal was struck whereby Dad could put his expertise to use in reconditioning some of the stock. The business prospered so much that by the time I came to know Albert well in the 1960s, he was still selling projectors to third world countries. He also told me a little story concerning the AJS. Apparently he had told the seller that he had found a 'grand lad' to buy the bike, so do him a good deal. It was one story that I didn't pass on to Dad.

Dick Hopkins had offered to take him to collect the AJS and knowing the village, they were soon knocking at the door. It was a case of 'love at first sight' when the outhouse door was opened to reveal the motorcycle with the registration number WU 6341; a West Riding number. They were informed it was a 350cc model 6 and being the bottom of the range, did not have lining on the petrol tank, that would have cost another £3. The seller must have had the same reasoning on economy as the Mellor family. There was also another concession when he announced that he was prepared to accept £20. So the sale was confirmed and as there was some petrol in the tank, it was only a matter of checking the tyres and starting, which Dad claimed it did with only a half dozen kicks. He was about to enter the age of modern motorcycling.

It must have been like a duck to water and he was soon conversant with all the controls. He was already looking forward to putting the 'AJ' through it's paces on a number of hills just to make a comparison with the performance of the Blackburne. He soon had his chance too, for they had to climb Harewood Bank between Harrogate and Leeds. It was not in the same class as Eccup or Arthington, but it featured a tight turn just before the top and if you had lost some speed before the bend, it would prove a good test for a 350cc side valve. It passed with flying colours and Dad had to ease off after the village of Harewood to allow Dick to catch up.

In the remaining months of 1926 the 'AJ' was to visit all the usual resorts on the east coast, along with two or three trips to Blackpool, one of which included a detour to Bowness on Windermere, which was to become a favourite for many years after. If the Blackburne had been worked hard, then the 'AJ' was going to be it's equal, even surpassing the performance when a single seat sidecar was attached.

In January,1927, they received notice to quit Lofthouse Hall. Demolition was planned to begin in August. Once again fate was to play a part in their future, for only a few weeks later they were advised by Leeds City Council that a house would become available to them from the last day of June. While that was extremely good news, they were now in a dilemma over the plans they were making for a trip to the T.T. Races, which included taking the AJS along. Their decision was that, with T.T. Week being early in the month and providing there were no changes in the dates they had been advised for moving, it should work out. The immediate problem, for Dad at least, was travelling to and from work. There had been a particularly heavy snowfall at the beginning of the month and he was compelled to using trams for transport which involved a change of routes too.

Spring finally came and the AJS was wheeled out for a first long run of the year. Mum had busied herself during the winter nights making the bookings for the holiday with the Isle of Man Steam Packet Company for themselves and motorcycle, along with a suitable guest house. A kennel holiday also had to be arranged for Queno von Brunanhoff! The first trip of the year just had to be Scarborough, if only to test the performance on Barton Hill and again the' AJ' made easy work of it. However, Joe on his Triumph Ricardo and Frank on his Scott just couldn't resist showing how it should be done by racing past well before the top.

It had been a good start to the year, for the Government had reduced the price of petrol to one shilling and four and a half pence (in old money of course). But there was even better news to come. In August the price dropped to one shilling and one penny (5½p) and don't forget we are talking in gallons (four and a half litres). This was the cheapest it had been since 1902. Before the big trip to the Island, Dad and Mum had a trip on their own to Bowness and followed this a week later with a first trip up Wharfedale on the AJS. This was their last outing before the holiday, enabling them to put some money aside and to allow for a major service before departure.

To the modern traveller, a trip from Leeds to Liverpool presents no difficulties. By joining the inner link road within minutes you are travelling along the M62 Motorway and assuming there are no hold ups, top gear can be maintained for the next sixty miles. But not so in 1927. It involved one of the most arduous journeys to undertake and was to remain so until the motorway was completed in the 1970s. There was no easy route out of Leeds. The Pennines gave you two options. The road to Huddersfield and over Standedge, then the grind through Oldham and Manchester, by which time you were around the halfway point. Then came the route over what were known as 'The Mosses' with names such as, Chat Moss, Bedford Moss and Glazebrook Moss. The list goes on until you reach Warrington then Widnes with a smokey aroma of varying industries. To complete the descriptive journey, there were the streets of Liverpool to be negotiated before arriving at the Pier Head.

I mentioned two options. The other led through Halifax and climbed over Rishworth Moor and Blackstone Edge to Rochdale and on through Manchester. In later years this road near to Halifax found fame when Percy Shaw had a 'bright idea' on his way home from the pub. His brain wave lives on as 'Cats Eyes' and made him a fortune.

They arrived with time to spare before the ferry sailed which gave them a chance to comply with the irritating rule that remaining petrol had to be drained from the tanks of all machines before lifting on board. Dad had also brought along an old sou'wester to protect the vulnerable parts against seawater. Having travelled the previous year, he had been aware that in a heavy sea, machines in the bow area were subject to a soaking. On this occasion, however, the sun was shining and conditions were near perfect and they both felt that this was where their motorcycling holiday was beginning. The return journey was seven days away.

With the AJS safely stowed on board they were ready to settle down for a relaxing voyage after the 80 miles tiring journey. They had been relieved of the burden of luggage as Dad's younger brother, Leslie and Mum's youngest brother, Tommy had booked to stay at Cunningham's Holiday Camp in Douglas and offered to carry an extra suitcase. Dad made a diary note that the ship was the 'Manx Maid,' adding it was the 'same old tub as last year.' It was an apt description too, for it served the I.O.M. Steam Packet Company for many years and was still in service when I first went to the Island in 1948. It gained a reputation for it's lively motion in heavy seas, which some seasoned travellers described as, "For the first two hours you think it is going to sink and for the next two you hope to hell it will!"

With the necessary paperwork completed during the voyage and just enough petrol in the carburettor, they headed to the first garage and a motorcycle holiday abroad. The guest house was easy to find and also boasted a spacious yard for parking, leaving the remainder of the day for just being holidaymakers. Although they had to first ensure their younger brothers had settled in despite them both being turned twenty. This was on the strict instruction from both their mothers!

Sunday began with Manx Kippers and ended with a ride around the T.T. course in an open sided char-a-banc. As it had already been reported that in practice Stanley Woods had pushed the lap record past the seventy mph barrier in the Senior class, they could both only marvel at such an achievement after seeing the twists and turns, along with bumps that were certainly testing the suspension on the coach. Even more gruelling was the climb out of Ramsey and by the time they reached the top and were heading towards the Bungalow, the radiator was showing a 'good head of steam.'

To watch the Junior T.T. on Monday they walked to Bray Hill and then on to Quarter Bridge. Freddie Dixon won on an HRD after a good race with H.J.Willis and Jimmy Simpson. The average speed over seven laps was 67.19mph, as fast as the 500cc race of a year earlier. Technology was advancing rapidly. On Tuesday they rode over to the west of the Island to explore the delights of Peel, Port Erin and Castletown before returning to Douglas. In the evening it was a 'bus man's holiday for Dad with a visit to the cinema to see a film which became one of his 'top ten' favourites. This was The Big Parade, featuring John Gilbert, then a big star but soon to fade into obscurity with the coming of sound. As they left the cinema, Dad congratulated the manager for a first class show, mentioning his connection with the cinema business. The publicity minded manager called out, "Come again and don't forget the name Strand."

Little did Dad know that in four years time, he would be joining the staff at a new cinema of that name and spend the next twenty five years there.

They made an early start on Wednesday. Many of the popular vantage points were taken well in advance, these were usually some of the slower bends which gave better views of riders and machines. Their plan was to reach Hillberry, which was a mile and a half from the finishing line. It was a fast downhill section that afforded good views of oncoming riders and if you kept to the outside of the course, you could move to another location easily. Dad tried taking some pictures, however, the box camera could not cope. But they had a packed lunch and a flask of tea prepared by their landlady to make an agreeable day.

Wal Handley on a Rex Acme dominated the Lightweight race, followed by one of the newcomers, L.Archangeli on a Moto Guzzi. Dad made a note that the Italian was using a screen mesh similar to the one Freddie Dixon had used in the Junior race. Although, unlike Freddie, he was racing with goggles.

Dad had naturally wanted to include a ride around the T.T. course while he had the opportunity, although Mum was not over enthusiastic. She thought it was a 'man' thing and was happy to let him have his moment of masculinity, especially as her brother, Tommy, had suggested going for a boat trip up the coast towards Laxey. Tommy collected Mum and they headed for the harbour. The first thing was to fill the AJS tank and then off to follow the John Bull and Dunlop markers and milestones. In later years he was always a little vague has to how many laps he completed. "A few." Would often be his answer. If I pushed him to a figure and said, "Less than ten?" He would just agree. But then the photograph turned up in 1957 following the death of younger brother, Leslie, who died at the early age of fifty. It was found by sister, Marjorie, who had known for many years that Leslie had accompanied Dad on the tour of the course. They had stopped just before Governor's Bridge for Leslie to take the picture. Grandmother Mellor had been somewhat protective of Leslie and never wanted him to have anything to do with cars or motorcycles so nothing was ever mentioned about the trip around the T.T. course.

The big race of the week, the Senior T.T. was always held on a Friday. Fastest in practice had been last year's winner, Stanley Woods and he was favourite to be the first rider to take consecutive wins, a feat that was later achieved for the first time in 1928 and 1929 by Charlie Dodson riding a Sunbeam. But Stanley was out of luck, although he did set up the fastest lap at 70.90mph. The race was won by Alec Bennett. After the racing and the roads were open for the public again Dad fired up the AJS. There was time before the evening meal for one last trip to Douglas Head and a chance to enjoy the magnificent view over the town, backed by Snaefell Mountain in the distance. Ironically, they were in the same spot where, some eight years later, George Formby shot a number of scenes in his classic film about the T.T. races, 'No Limit.'

Friday evening was when Mum took over. Preparation and packing were her speciality and as the first sailing on Saturday was 9am; it would mean an early start. Breakfast was from 6.30am; and they ensured they were among the first down. Leslie had collected their suitcase and Dad had checked over the AJS, so they were on the quayside before 8am. The day was dull with just a slight breeze so the crossing should be reasonably smooth. In later years when recalling the return trip, he mentioned his apprehension of the ride back through industrial Lancashire and in particular negotiating the streets of Manchester on a Saturday. But once they were back in Liverpool and he was hearing the steady beat of the side valve exhaust, the miles seemed to fall away. One memory he loved retelling about the journey when crossing from Lancashire into Yorkshire and from one of the highest points, was seeing the whole of the West Riding lit by the late afternoon sun. He would sometimes add one of his many philosophical sayings about 'memories lasting longer than dreams.' It was just one of many that I grew up with.

It was back to the work routine on the Monday and other than being used for trips to and from work, the AJS saw little in the way of long journeys. Now they had to prepare for the house move. They had both noticed a change in the behaviour of the dog, that sixth sense so often found in animals appeared to be aware of forthcoming changes which had of course started with a week in kennels. A week before the move they decided to take Que to see the new house and acquaint him with the area, which meant taking two tram journeys.

As they were walking up the path to the door, a Jack Russell terrier came from around the rear of the house with a stick in it's mouth and was probably expecting them to throw it for him. Que beat them to it. He grabbed hold of the stick and with the terrier still attached, began twirling round in obvious fun. That wasn't how the dog's owner saw it and she shrieked with alarm for them to call off the dog. So instead of a gentle introduction to the new surroundings, they had to beat a hasty retreat back to the tram stop.

There were going to be other changes too which perhaps the dog had sensed. Mum had a check up with the doctor and to her total surprise was told that she was expecting. The happy event was going to be in September so the move was taking place at the right time. They were leaving two rooms and a kitchen and as they had not yet acquired much in the way of furniture, it did not require a large van for the removal. This meant Dad could travel with the driver, while Mum and Que would follow by tram and by the time she arrived every thing had been unloaded. From the moment she got off the tram, the dog knew the route to take and on arrival and going into the house, the first thing it did was to run upstairs. In a moment of laughter Dad wondered if it was checking the windows in case there came a time when it had to leap out again!

They now had somewhere they could call home and being only a couple of miles from the cinema, Dad went back to cycling. It was a simple equation of fitness and saving money. For the remainder of the summer months every chance was taken of making a trip into the local countryside, usually by tram or bus. Joe Buckler had bought a movie camera and used the occasions to make little action films which would now be of great personal family interest. Did they survive the war I wonder?

On the second day of September, 1927, a son was born to Dad and Mum and given the name, Ronald. As is the way with many families, this was the name he retained until early teens, it then being for ever after shortened to Ron. For the immediate future the AJS was to see very little use, other than solo trips about the town. It was certainly low mileage when purchased and the next two or three years were not going to add significantly to this.

The end of the twenties were turbulent years. In October, 1929 came the Wall Street crash from which many ordinary workers were to feel the effect of, mainly from wage reductions, or worse still unemployment. The word redundancy was not in common usage then. Dad was asked to take a cut in wages with a promise of better things to come. For him it couldn't have come at a worse time, although Herbert, the assistant operator was still single and better able to ride out the difficulties. Grandfather Mellor was also in difficulties with his film rental business, which a few months later were added to when he received a compulsory purchase order on his house. The whole area was to be demolished and replaced with a Civic Hall to be opened by King George V and Queen Mary in 1933. There is a twist of irony in all this when the man responsible for the title of this book would be standing yards from where Dad had kept the Blackburne to deliver his opening speech.

As noted in earlier pages, throughout this period of commercial and domestic strife, the cinemas of Britain were a haven of relief for those caught up in the financial backlash. And to ease their woes they were now enticed with such advertising claims as 'An all singing and dancing production' now that we had 'talking pictures'. So it was with some trepidation that both Dad and his assistant, Herbert, answered a call to the owner's office one morning in 1930. Fearing the worst they pondered the possible reasons. Another reduction in wages was one. Unemployment with the closure of the cinema was dismissed as unlikely in view of the continuing ticket sales, but it might be a request to work longer hours for the same wages, a not uncommon ploy used by employers at this period. That knock on the door was to bring changes for both of them.

Laid out on the desk were a number of plans and drawings to which the owner beckoned, adding, "I vant you the take a look at deese." His English had only marginally improved in the last five years. Fortunately his son, being born and educated in England, was to continue with the reason for the meeting. They had purchased a plot of land in Hunslet, about a mile from the present cinema and the plan was to open another cinema to be known as 'The Strand'. Not unnaturally, Dad's mind wandered back to the night at the Strand Cinema in Douglas, Isle of Man, and to the cheery greeting from the manager. The son continued, "We want you, Tom, to take over when it's completed and for Herbert to be 'Chief' here. Then came the icing on the cake! Their wages were to be restored to the amount they were before the cuts of 1929 and they would pay for a sidecar to be fitted to the AJS which could be used for collecting films. There was also a cherry on top! There would be a £1 rise for both of them. While that may appear risible to the modern reader, let me take a moment to illustrate what that meant to the working man of almost ninety years ago.

A new 325 x 19 front tyre was 27 shillings (£1.35p). The tube would cost you five shillings (25p). A pair of footrest rubbers would be one shilling and sixpence (7½p) and remember, these were not cheap foreign imports but made in Leicester by John Bull. A good road map on linen would be around two shillings (10p). So when the meeting ended there was much to be considered. Having a sidecar meant whole new horizons now he was a family man and he knew just the man to see. This was Harold Barrett, a small suburban dealer who dealt in second hand machines and repairs and who would expand rapidly in the years after world war two with premises in Kirkstall Road, Leeds. It was Harold who had originally sold Dad the Blackburne.

The new cinema opened late in 1931 and it was into the New Year before Harold had a suitable sidecar for fitting. The accompanying invoice will provide another illustration of 1930s prices relating to motorcycling. The little 350cc AJS that had once covered the T.T. course was now to become a true workhorse. Joe Buckler's family had expanded so he was now running an outfit with a child/adult sidecar. Dick Hopkins had yet to start a family and was still loyal to Triumph, but now with a 1931 Model NSD fitted with a 550cc side valve engine. A perfect model to be attached to a sidecar in due course. Frank Buckler had moved over to 4-wheels but joined them occasionally at some of the local beauty spots. Even Herbert, now promoted to Chief Operator, had moved on to a 1929 BSA Sloper and would sometimes join them. His model was supplied without lights, which at the time would have cost more than his pocket could meet, so it meant he had to make sure he set off for home in good time.

The AJS was of course still fitted with acetylene lamps with the need to keep a tin of carbide handy. On one occasion when leaving Scarborough later than planned, Dad realised the situation was dire when he discovered his spare tin was almost empty. As the sun was still above the horizon, he knew he could reach Malton where there was a garage that still stocked supplies of carbide. What he did not expect was a long queue of traffic due to an accident, and now no longer being a solo motorcycle was at a disadvantage. Time ticked by as they moved in stops and starts with the sun gradually sinking lower in the sky. Throughout all this, Ron was fast asleep on Mum's knee, seemingly oblivious to the clatter of open valve gear. I was later told that I was just as docile when my turn came to occupy the knee. The only difference being, instead of the clatter of Wolverhampton valve gear, I tolerated a similar noise manufactured at Small Heath!

They were now well behind time and as they came into Malton the time was showing a quarter past ten and the garage was in darkness. They had ridden in convoy so far with Joe at the front and Dick at the rear, but now they were well past lighting up time. The house attached to the garage was in darkness, save for a small glow from the highest room, which suggested a candle. At least the door was fitted with a hefty knocker that would arouse anyone from the attic room. Dad rapped three or four times then looked upwards. The light was still showing. "Try harder", said Dick. Who, with Joe was standing some distance away, as if leaving Dad to receive any wrath from a tired and testy garage proprietor. So he tried harder. This time the glow moved. It passed a lower window, then an even lower window until there was the sound of bolts being withdrawn.

"Now for it", said Dick as if preparing to run. A man appeared with a candle, dressed in a nightshirt with an overcoat thrown over his shoulders. Dad explained the situation and that he needed a tin of 'Globri' carbide, the sixpenny size!

"I shall have to charge you double," said the prickly owner. "Take it or leave it."

Dad was probably thinking of one of his regular philosophic epigrams about needs must etc; etc; so he reluctantly agreed. It took around ten minutes to generate a gas flow and with a brilliant front and rear light they were able to complete the remaining miles. Amazingly, Ron was still sleeping through it all. Next day he recounted the incident to his boss about having to pay double. As previously mentioned he was a Russian Jew who had now adopted the name, Cohen. All he said was, "Vell business is business!"

During the summer of 1933, Mum had been to see the doctor and again came away with some news for Dad, namely, he was going to be a dad again! The expected date was mid-April. But before the happy event arrived there was a death in the family. Champion Queno von Brunanhoff contracted an internal organ decease and died before they were able to contact a Vet. He was nine years old. Obviously they were both very upset. Dad had raised and trained him from a six month old puppy, while for Mum, he had been her constant and protective companion during all the lonely evenings at Lofthouse Hall.

1934 was an arduous year for the family, in addition to my arrival! Grandfather Mellor had received very little in the way of compensation for losing his house. The major film rental companies were muscling in on much of his territory and he was owed a considerable amount of money from many of the smaller cinemas, including the one Dad was employed by. It was going to take some delicate negotiations to resolve the matter at the centre of which was a BSA Blue Star fitted with a sports sidecar.

The problems began on a Wednesday in September. Dad had parked the AJS combination outside the cinema, having just returned from the railway station after collecting the new film programme. Old Mr Cohen, the name he was now known by, was coming down the road in his rather elderly and antiquated Bean 14hp open tourer. He could only be described as an occasional motorist, much preferring the simpler mode of transport by tramcar and of course we are talking of the days before a driving test was required. He also had the belief that, other than a gallon of petrol now and then, the car needed little else. Apparent on this day when he needed brakes!

By a remarkable coincidence of incalculable odds, coming the other way was Grandfather Mellor accompanied by a film salesman colleague on their way to meet Mr Cohen. They were not only eye witnesses, they had a 'grandstand' view of the whole incident. It was clear that Mr Cohen's car had a braking fault or inefficient brakes, or a combination of the two. It struck the AJS head on and turned it over, the sidecar wheel collapsing under the impact. The runaway was only brought to a halt when it collided with a street lamp, with the sidecar body taking the brunt of the crash.

Dad had heard the collision and rushed out to find the aftermath with old Mr Cohen standing in the road wringing his hands and calling, "wot'll I do, wot'll I do." This just happened to be the title of a popular song of the day.

The gas lamp was leaning at an angle with the mantle broken and a flame several inches long shooting skywards. But there was yet more to come and this is where the story really begins! The film salesman was also a special constable and experienced in taking situations under control. His first action was to arrange for one of the cinema staff to telephone the gas company to arrange for the main supply to be turned off. Then when making a cursory check of the car, he noticed the Road Fund Licence card, the name by which it was then known, was out of date. It was time to adjourn to the manager's office. Mr Cohen knew he was in trouble. He was probably already fearing adverse newspaper publicity far greater than that generated by the 'Nellie on the bench' commotion.

But there were at least five hours before the start of the first house showing, time enough to try and come to an amicable arrangement. First and foremost he accepted all liability and agreed to replace Dad's machine with a new model and suitable sidecar. Then realising that Grandfather was a leading witness, he also agreed to settle all outstanding invoices. There would also be a bill coming from the Gas Company for repairs and replacements.

The film salesman was also a key witness and having to play two roles. He was making notes of all the arrangements using the cinema's letter heading, with carbon paper inserted for copies to be made available. But wearing his salesman hat, perhaps he too would be hoping for an order for his wares and old Mr Cohen may well have seen the wisdom in placing business with his company. That is only an assumption on my part for Dad only told me this story in later years, fifty years later in fact, when both the Cohens, father and son, had passed away. Nor was there any mention of the happening in his diaries for this period. It seems discretion was another of his virtues.

With autumn approaching the windows of the local dealers were taken up with news of the forthcoming models for the 1935 season. Dad was already thinking in terms of economy, probably based on his natural penny-wise doctrine along with his familiarity of how well the 350cc AJS had coped with a single seat sidecar attached. He may also have been easing the pain for his boss who was paying for the new outfit. There was certainly a wide choice of models with AJS and BSA the front runners and it was only decided when the BSA dealer was able to offer a better price with a sidecar of BSA manufacture fitted. The total cost came to £64. There was now another matter under consideration also. With an expanding family, Grandfather Mellor was urging him to buy his own house, suggesting he looked at some of the new developments taking place on the edges of the City boundaries, even producing a selection of brochures for an area that Dad was familiar with. But before that there was the matter of a BSA with a single seat sidecar to be attended to.

Delivery of the 350cc Blue Star model could not be guaranteed before March which meant going back to cycling and tram journeys. But following several bus journeys to one of the new fringe developments, he took probably the biggest decision of his life. Having looked at a number of plots, they selected a cul-de-sac location which at this stage only consisted of pegs and white tape. You had to imagine the rest was a 3-bedroom semi-detached house. Nevertheless, a mortgage was agreed based on a purchase price of £500 which of course was a princely sum in 1935 when the average wage was around £6 per week. But an even more staggering statistic shows the sale price 79 years later in 2014, had risen to £225.000.

It was May before the BSA Blue Star was delivered and it was given the Leeds Registration, BNW 275. However, as the new house was not quite ready to move into and only having a single wicket gate at the current address, the BSA was stored in the rarely used crush hall that ran alongside the cinema. The first trip out was to collect the new film programme from the station, plus a deviation to show off the new purchase to Dick Hopkins then to see Herbert and leave his forthcoming programme of films. Mum had her first ride in the new sidecar a few days later when they went to collect a new addition to the family. This was an Irish Red Setter puppy, apparently without a lengthy parentage for she was given the very undistinguished name of Betty.

My first wheels were in the form of a pushchair and I am told I displayed much puzzlement as I watched the furniture disappearing from each room and into a removal van. Nor could I probably understand why, after a lengthy journey by bus and push chair, all my favourite playthings were waiting for me. Obviously, at this age I have no recollections of events so I am constantly referring to Dad's diary notes as to my first ventures related to motorcycles. It would seem to have been around the age of sixteen months when I find a mention of a trip to a stately home on the outskirts of Leeds. Temple Newsam had been acquired by the City Corporation in 1922 and was set in over 900 acres of parkland. It was also within easy reach of both grand parents, so was to become a regular place for walks and picnics.

There is more definite confirmation at the age of eighteen months with a photograph taken on the beach at Scarborough, this shows the 'Blue Star' in the background and by the time we are into 1936 there are regular diary entries of trips to the east coast along with one to Blackpool and it is noted that by the end of the year, the mileage is recorded as 1496.

1936 had started with the Nation plunged into mourning following the death of King George V. The following period of turmoil and upheaval within the Royal Household has been so frequently documented it makes any further mention superfluous, other than to mention that Dad often regarded this time as a watershed in the Nation's general economy after some twelve years of depression, austerity and industrial disquiet. At last it seemed that prices were becoming stable and the workforce began to feel that there was a permanency with each job application.

As a motorcycling family we now had a pecking order. Brother Ron was ten years old and fully competent as a pillion rider, although he never missed an opportunity of a car ride on the occasions when Frank Buckler joined the party. As he grew up sporting activities occupied his life and other than a brief encounter with the pedal cycle, he never acquired a driving licence for a motorcycle or car. As for me, my position was still the 'knee' and being indoctrinated by BSA tappet rattle, or so I like to assure myself. In later years I was told of one of my inquisitive finger pointing was often at the BSA 'piled arms' trade mark on the petrol tank and I have to confess to this day that I still think the Company stylists got it wrong in placing it there.

With only two more summers left before the world, and certainly Britain changed forever, at least that was the view of both parents, there were still regular weekend outings both to the coast and to inland scenic attractions. Again I have to rely on parental reminiscences about the occasion I was allowed to sit in the sidecar alone while Mum took the pillion seat. It seems while passing through York on the way to visiting friends, each time we had to stop at traffic lights or other holdups, I was telling passing pedestrians where we were going. While that may not seem too unusual for a three year old, I was wearing the goggles I had been bought for my last birthday, even though the sidecar was fitted with a full screen.

On May 12, 1937, with all the pomp and ceremony of time-honoured tradition, King George V1 and Queen Elizabeth were crowned at Westminster Abbey. For the nation it gave some small respite from the ever growing gloom of daily news reports as Statesmen dashed to and fro between London and various European Capitals trying to ward off the threat of war. There were already rumours of plans to ration food and petrol supplies at a time when the price of a gallon had reached one shilling and seven pence (8p). As if this was not worrying enough there were plans to issue all children with gas masks. For Dad and Mum they had seen it all before in 1914 but were now faced with not only their own well being but that of their ageing parents. But the sun shone and the Blue Star, now fully run in, performed as well as ever with Dad boasting about it was a 'tickle-starter'. For the two summers leading up to the outbreak of world war two, there were fewer trips to Scarborough or indeed the east coast in general and I suspect this may have been Mum's apprehension to the possibility of a repeat action of the German's shelling the town in December 1914.

The diary for the period mentions regular trips to Bowness, along with some other popular Lake District locations and of course Blackpool was not forgotten. The annual week's holiday in 1938 was taken there and I have a vague memory of the bedroom window of the boarding house being within feet of a railway line. Sadly I had not yet reached the 'train spotting' period of my boyhood. I was told in later years that as a family, we were looked upon by the other guests as 'well to do,' as we had travelled by road. Whereas, the others had all come by train. Such is the strange trait of 'pigeon holing' by the English. On the return journey there would have been the now traditional 'pip' on the horn as we passed the signpost to Mellor on the outskirts of Blackburn but there is also a diary note about colliding with a dog that dashed into the road.

Whenever Dad related this story, it was always embellished with a little humour to emphasise that the dog came to no real harm. It was struck by the nose of the sidecar and did a flip somersault onto the pavement whereupon it barked furiously at Dad before disappearing into a gateway.

For a five year old, the opening weeks of 1939 were no different from others I had toddled into. There always seemed to be snow at this time but I had not yet inherited the family sledge. This was still the preserve of older brother, Ron, and as is the way with older brothers he was reluctant to share the pleasures with a younger nuisance. If our parents were worried about the preparations for war, it was never openly revealed even though our radio, which played a huge part in our social life, was always switched on. Dad of course was always missing in the evenings, which gave rise to a popular joke amongst the families of cinema projectionists. It went something like.

Small boy. "Mummy, who is that strange man that comes in late at night?"

Mother. "That isn't a strange man dear, that's your Daddy."

So there was much talk of conscription, air raid shelters, evacuation and identity cards that would have to be carried by everyone.

Reference to the diary for the year shows two trips to Blackpool in July and August, but the earlier months seem to have been confined to local pleasure attractions, including Temple Newsam, where I caused a domestic rumpus by falling in the ornamental fish pond. This huge expanse of parkland became a favourite picnic spot for many of the families who worked in the local cinema business and in those final months before Britain's ultimatum to Germany expired, Dad often commented that on some Sunday's there where three dozen cars and motorcycles in the group. In another thirty or so years, I would come to know many of them in the autumn of their lives and yet I have no clear recollection of this period, save for one very important announcement that came over the radio one Sunday morning on the 3rd. September, 1939. Whenever I hear a recording of the speech I still have a feeling of uneasy dread.

From the outbreak of war petrol was rationed which meant that all road users had to apply for their allowance of coupons. These were issued as units according to horse power or c.c. in the case of motorcycles. One unit equalled one gallon of fuel and they were only valid for one month to prevent people hoarding them. It was a meagre concession that curtailed any outings for pleasure. Day trips to the seaside were now becoming futile as many of the resorts on the east coast were now being prepared for invasion threats with miles of barbed wire, concrete blocks and various other means of thwarting landing craft. This in turn effected many of the commercial outlets that relied upon the holiday maker or day tripper. 'Closed for the duration' became a common attachment to awnings and windows along sea fronts around Britain. On the west coast, Blackpool in particular, many hotels and guest houses were commandeered by the military.

As if to add to the hardship, all lighting on vehicles had to be restricted, or masked to an official design from the Home Office. The light shown was dismal and with an added danger of blacked out street lamps, there was a marked increase in night time accidents. For Dad this made life difficult as his job did not usual finish until 10.30pm. and with a 7 mile journey to contend with, some along rural roads, the Blue Star saw little use. By the end of 1941 the mileage reading was just over 7000.

Then to help the war effort and farmers the Government introduced Double Summertime which extended daylight until after 11pm. However, this was of no help to those who might wish to extend their use of a vehicle for in March 1942, the Government announced that the basic civilian petrol ration was to be abolished. Fuel would now only be available to 'official' users such as emergency services, bus companies, farmers and doctors. A red dye was added to petrol and use of this fuel was an offence. The actor and composer, Ivor Novello was jailed for thirty days for the mis-use of fuel. Dad's boss tried to apply for an exemption, claiming the need was to collect film programmes from the railway station. A Whitehall letter told him in no uncertain terms to use the tram!

So with just over 7000 miles on the speedometer in around seven years, the Blue Star was sheeted over in a corner of the cinema crush hall where patrons had no access. It would be almost three years before the wheels would turn again, although the engine was regularly turned over and Dad had also devised some wooden blocks to lift the tyres clear of the concrete flooring. Occasionally, I would be allowed to lift the sheeting and polish the tank, giving special attention to the lovely BSA green panels, a shade of green I have rarely seen reproduced correctly in present day restoration projects.

2:   1945 to 1966

With an end to hostilities in Europe and a Labour Government in power with an absolute and overwhelming majority for the first time in Britain's history, petrol restrictions for civilians were eased but it would be another five years before rationing ended completely. A new Act of Parliament, the 1948 Motor Spirit Act ruled that red dye in fuel was for commercial vehicles only and a private car driver could lose his licence for a year if this was found in his car. A petrol station could be closed down if they sold the fuel to a private motorist.

I was now of an age where I understood much of what was happening around the family.

No longer did Mum have to spell out words to other relatives whenever I was within earshot. So I was to become conversant when listening to Dad and his pals relating the various methods suggested in removing the red dye from the commercial fuel. The popular one for many years after was to strain the petrol through the carbon filter of a gas mask and as these were now redundant, there was a ready supply. But there were many more theories which we tried as I was nearing motorcycle licence age. I already owned a third share in a 1929 Raleigh which was kept in a local farmer's barn and having failed to get any results with lighter fuel we conducted our own 'scientific' experiments.

The current favourite, told to us by the mechanic at the local garage, involved straining through a loaf of bread and the mouldier the bread the better. It didn't work, nor I hasten to add, did the gas mask filter. Then there was the paraffin plan. This meant buying a gallon of paraffin, mixing it with the petrol, then trying to drop the temperature to near freezing. What was supposed to happen was the paraffin would absorb the dye, leaving the petrol to be poured off. The bonus being you could still use the paraffin in a heater so there was no loss involved.

Someone came up with the idea that submerging in deep water would be the closest we could get to freezing and as we lived near a fair sized reservoir, a plan was hatched. Rope was plentiful after the war, being used in many areas of industry, so a suitable length was attached to the can and it was floated out on a plank and given a tug when about twenty feet away. All this happened on a Sunday when there were no maintenance staff about, so it meant waiting a week before we could assess the results of our research. A more learned mind would probably have said, "Don't hold your breath." But at fourteen you can hardly be judged as 'streetwise,' at least not in Leeds in 1948.

We returned a week later and hauled out the can and headed for the barn discussing the possibility of becoming rich and how we would spend the money. What came out was red! "It needs to separate." was the first suggestion. So we waited. And waited. Two days went by without any significant change in the liquid. Someone said why not try it in the Raleigh and I found myself sitting astride. Being the only one who's father had a motorcycle did give one a commanding position and at least I had some idea of the purpose of the controls. The engine fired up and ran perfectly. Then the smoke started. It came out of every possible joint from cylinder head to the crankcase breather with the exhaust providing the major out-pouring. I engaged a gear and started off down the field disappearing into the bottom corner and out of sight of my fellow-shareholders. They knew the engine was still running by the clouds of smoke still being emitted, but it was now becoming darker and there was a strong smell of paraffin. Going back up the field left me with one of those moments that remain with you always. Even as I recall it now there is a clarity of the day with all it's detail. The smell, the smoke that hung in the air with no breeze to chase away the evidence of our controlled test and the slightly smug satisfaction as I handed over to my pal with a feeling of, 'that's the way you do it.' Yes life was good in 1948.

But I have allowed my own entry into the narrative to take us too far ahead in time. Back in 1945 a basic petrol ration did have limitations. Using the Blue Star to travel to and from work was not an efficient way of using your supply and with no undercover protection at the house meant the still almost pristine condition would suffer. There were other factors too. Joe Buckler was now a car owner and with brother, Frank, was running an engineering business which left no time for trips to the seaside. Mum, too, was beginning to feel that the war years had changed her life. Now there seemed to be less time for social occasions. Her eldest son, Ron, would soon be receiving his 'calling up papers'. Her youngest son, me, was soon to leave the infants school which was only walking distance away and move to a senior school which would mean a daily bus fare. Riding in a sidecar just did not seem to hold the allure of previous years.

So back under the sheet in the crush hall went the Blue Star and for the next year or so it was only used for local town work. Young Mr Cohen was now running two cinemas and as he had not learnt to drive, it became his chauffeur ridden transport, much in the way of his father before him. With the ending of hostilities and a meagre supply of petrol available, many tired-out motorcycles began to appear again, often at a premium price if it was still in running order. One such machine that came to light just around the corner from the cinema was an OK Supreme fitted with a 250cc JAP side valve engine. Dad recalled, "It was not much to look at but it was fitted with a Burman 4-speed gearbox." He bought it for £8.

Needless to say it took several days to bring it back to running order, whereupon it was soon evident that the timing side main bearing bush was very badly worn. It was to be my introduction to the inner workings of a motorcycle engine and I became fascinated with how simple it all looked to be. One of the evening attendants at the cinema had a day job at the Hunslet Engine Company, which was only a few hundred yards from the cinema.

He not only produced a drift to remove the bush, but made a three legged puller for removing the necessary sprockets. I still have them and have used both on many occasions down the years. The sturdy little machine was soon back on the road and giving good value for each gallon of petrol. I have always had a fetish for registration numbers from early school days and at that age was able to quote most of the towns and borough councils that issued them. The OK Supreme was issued with DKH 207 by the Borough of Kingston-upon-Hull in April, 1937.

Much of my mis-spent youth was in cinema projection boxes or in the family complimentary seat on the back row so my formative years centred very much around films and film stars. This did have it's rewards at school though, where I was able to swop much sought after film frame clips for whatever might be of use to me. For the boys it would be, Betty Grable, Rita Hayworth and Maureen O'Hara. For the girls, Humphrey Bogart, Cary Grant and Errol Flynn were their heartthrobs.

This meant I would race home from school, down a hastily prepared tea and then off on the pillion for two performances of the latest release and with luck, a Laurel and Hardy or a Three Stooges Comedy. By the age of twelve I was proficient in rewinding each reel as it ran off, changing the advertising slides after counting to thirty and starting the gramophone to play the latest 'pop' song on a 78rpm record as the patrons left the cinema. Then back on the pillion in the dark, keeping a wary eye for tram passengers who boarded and alighted by crossing from the pavement into the road. For all this knowledge I received two shillings a night, which I often thought was paid from Dad's pocket and not Mr Cohen's! Looking back at this period, the little OK Supreme lived up to it's name. Heading north out of the centre of Leeds there was quite a climb after leaving the tram tracks at Sheepscar and heading towards Scot Hall Road. If the traffic lights were in your favour and you were able to have a running start, this gave an obvious advantage, but if baulked, then it would be a slower climb. I came to appreciate that when I started work at fifteen and cycled the same route.

1946 brought new horizons in my world of motorcycles which began with an introduction to road racing. I had often overheard stories of the exploits of Woods, Handley, Guthrie or Dixon and how they tackled bends with such gripping names as, The Goose neck, Kate's Cottage, Signpost Corner and Bray Hill. A day trip to Scarborough was planned, on this occasion by train, to see the inaugural meeting at the Oliver's Mount circuit. From that moment I was 'hooked' with the never to be forgotten first wiff of Castrol R, the open megaphone exhaust and the way the riders crouched and leaned and changed gear and slipped the clutch all in one blurring moment. The earlier names were Dad and Mum's heroes, mine were to become, Parkinson, Jefferies, Archer, Frith, Daniell and Cann. From that day at Oliver's Mount in 1946 how could I ever have known that thirty or so years into the future, Dennis Parkinson, Alan Jefferies and Maurice Cann would feature in my life with motorcycles being the common factor.

Another motorcycle highlight occurred in 1947 and once again the memories live on to this day. It began when Mum was invited to spend a week in London with a cousin, who had a relative through marriage that lived just a short journey on the Underground from the centre. A trip to the Capital in 1947 was not something you took lightly. For Mum it meant weeks of preparation and how were the menfolk going to cope? There were only two of us at this time, Brother Ron was away on National Service with the Royal Navy.

It was Dad who solved the problem. He would book his weeks holiday and we would go off on a tour of the Yorkshire Dales on the OK Supreme. A whole week of Father and Son bonding culminating with a visit to see Grandfather and Grandmother Mellor who had now moved to West Hartlepool as Grandfather had taken over the Gaiety Cinema. This was truly a family business as, Son, Leslie worked in the projection box, daughter, Marjorie worked in the pay kiosk and Grandfather was front of house welcoming the patrons.

The machine preparation was to be my first enrolment into the true mechanics of motorcycling. Perhaps now it would be called 'spannerman', but back then it was more a case of 'hold this', 'pass that', or just watch where the grease gun was applied or how brake and clutch cables are adjusted, chains and tyres checked and a general tightening of nuts and bolts, with a special emphasis on mudguard stays, one of his pet abominations. In the earlier days of an almost rigid ride, fracture through vibration was a constant cause of delay.

The final planning was the route and once again this was to be the commencement of a fascination with maps that remains to this day. A good folding map of Yorkshire was obtained (which I still have) and studied carefully to ensure we filled the week with visits to as many worthwhile centres of interest, either historic, scenic or scientific. These covered my top subjects at school.

We were off by mid-morning on the first Saturday and heading north through Harrogate and Knaresborough towards Boroughbridge, our first planned stop. It was to see the Roman remains, along with the huge stone obelisks known as 'The Devils Arrows' the origin of which has long been debated. However, the Mosaic floor was a beautifully preserved example which regrettably our black and white film was unable to convey. After lunch we were back on the road and now heading west towards Ripon, Pateley Bridge and Grassington, our first overnight stop. On the way we made a quick stop to look at the well preserved ruins of Fountains Abbey, then on towards Pateley Bridge where the first hard work for the OK Supreme was to begin. Although I was not aware of it at the time, I am sure Dad welcomed the 4-speed Burman gearbox as there were some tough climbs ahead. Greenhow Hill was the first test and taken in style, in fact we had intended stopping at Stump Cross Caverns, but the little 'OK' was going so well, Dad decided to keep going until we were over the summit and having an easy ride down into Wharfedale for our Bed and Breakfast stop in Grassington.

Before setting off next morning, I was given my first lesson of the tour. As we were now in the real Dales with some steep grades ahead, he thought he should increase the oil supply and after starting the engine, asked me to count the drops from the beak of the Pilgrim pump. Fascinated, I watched each drop disappear, not then realising that here was the life 'blood' of the engine and should never be ignored. He made it around 30 drops per minute and thought 40 would be safer, adding, 'better to have too much than too little.'

Dad of course knew Wharfedale well. I had cycled with him as far as Otley but for me this was new ground, however, I too was soon to fall under it's charm and would in later years cover many miles following the River Wharfe from it's source to where it spills into the Ouse a mere ten miles from my present home. The journey up the Dale on this Sunday morning would be hard to imagine for the present day tourist. Now in summer months it is a constant flow of traffic in both directions and there are regular touring coaches to contend with.

We passed very few cars in either direction and except for several cycling clubs had the road to ourselves. Another vast difference for the present day motorcyclist was being able to communicate with your pillion passenger. As the little side valve burbled along, we were able to talk almost normally. But I may be doing an injustice to the modern rider as todays technology has given us the intercom and perhaps they are chattering away to each other inside their helmets.

We were soon approaching Kilnsey with the dramatic overhanging crag alongside us and where, in four years time, I would be riding in the field opposite in one of my early grass track race meetings. I am never sure of the word to use. Is it fate or destiny? But there would be a number of other incidents and places during the week where I would be brought back to in later years through following my chosen path of life.

Now we were passing Kettlewell, a true Dales village and little changed in the intervening years. Climbing away to the right is the fearsome Park Rash hill with all it's memories of success and failure. For many years the repair garage by the bridge over a narrowing River Wharfe, was owned by Dick Wilkinson, one of my competitors on the grass and of course the father of Bill Wilkinson, renowned International trials rider and the last man to win The Scottish 6-Day Trial on a British machine in 1969.

Now the Dale was narrowing and we were climbing, evident from the note of the exhaust. I had now become familiar with the sequence of gear changing, but Dad was having to hold lower gears for longer as the climb steepened. We were heading for the top of Fleet Moss when Dad shouted we were around 2000 feet above sea level. In my juvenile innocence I asked if it was higher than Blackpool Tower. The view from the top was impressive. To the north could be seen hills in Northumberland while away to the west Ingleborough dominated the scene, which the map indicated the summit at 2373 feet. On the western horizon the hills of the Lake District stood out against the late afternoon sun.

The condition of the road surface had worsened and as it now dropped steeply towards Hawes, Dad thought it best to proceed with caution. He calculated we had about another twenty miles to cover and with the engine now rested, we set off at a tickover speed as he weaved amongst the loose stones, trying to pick the smoothest, and safest route.

We were now dropping down into Wensleydale, which my geography teacher had taught me was the only Yorkshire Dale without a River to it's name. Again I was unaware that the area was to become familiar in the 1950s through grass track racing at a number of Dales Shows which have been traditional in the area for many years past. The little town of Hawes on this day was in complete contrast to what the 21st century visitor would find. Then it had a railway station that linked the King's Cross to Edinburgh line in the east to the Leeds to Glasgow line in the west, then known as, and still is, The Settle and Carlisle Railway. There were few cars about and even fewer motorcycles. Unlike the scene today when it is sometimes swamped with the modern biker. A name I deplore but use if only to distinguish them from motorcyclists of my generation.

We took the road towards Ingleton, passing under the Settle and Carlisle line at Ribblehead Viaduct, just as an express was heading north. I had now added the steam locomotive to my list of hobbies, marvelling at the wonderful mechanical motions and sheer size of every component. Ingleborough now seemed to be towering above us as we came into the hamlet of Chapel-le-Dale and Dad slowed in front of the largest of the cluster of houses. This was the Hill Inn and a sign in the window advertised, Bed & Breakfast. Unbeknown to me, he had arranged accommodation for two nights.

Our room looked straight up at the northern slope of the mountain and from the window it looked an easy enough climb. With two hours before the evening meal we ventured out to try. The exuberance of youth was obviously greater than my stamina and I soon decided it was steeper than it looked and headed back down, possibly swayed by the thought of food.

Dad had prepared a list of possible places to visit, two of which were below ground. White Scar Cave and Weathercote Cave, the latter just happened to be within walking distance of the Hill Inn. Weathercote was an intriguing fissure that disappeared into the ground with just a simple gate across the entrance. It was to be my first sighting of stalagmites and stalactites, daunting at first before the eyes grew accustomed to the restricted light, then a truly wonderful scene that could only be marvelled at.

We set off towards Ingleton the intention being to walk to the waterfalls at Thornton Force and Pecca. Dad had last visited here in the early thirties with the AJS combination and before Brother Ron had started school, so for him it really was a trip down memory lane. In the afternoon and on our way back to the Hill Inn, we stopped to visit White Scar Cave. Not too many years ago I drove past the site and was astonished at the changes that tourism had brought to the surroundings. In 1947 there was no electricity below ground and all illumination was by candle and small battery torches. It did though make the underground lake look spooky. At the time I had a passing interest in fishing and as I was constantly being reminded by my parents to speak out and ask questions to open the conversation, I enquired of the guide if there was any fish in the lake?

"I don't know I have never fished in it." was his reply. I have never been convinced that asking a question is a good conversation opener!

Back at the car park two other motorcyclists had arrived, they too were on a touring holiday from Scotland. As motorcyclists do, they were soon in conversation with Dad while I just stood listening. I couldn't understand a word they were saying!

For the evening's pre dinner stroll, we decided to go in the opposite direction, across the road down to the stream that flowed towards Ingleton. Later study of our map showed this was the River Doe that flowed into the River Greta, which then flowed into the River Lune and on into Morecambe Bay. Little tributaries were just another of his foibles that rubbed off on me. When the meal was finished, I provided the other guests with some amusement when the waitress asked would anyone like the last piece of apple pie. It was my voice that piped up.

It had rained heavily during the night but was fine by the time we were ready to leave. The 'OK' had been parked under cover and was soon up and running. Today would see us travel across the country to the coast and over into Durham, a first for me, although Dad and Mum had previously visited Grandfather Mellor by train. We headed back into Hawes for petrol then a short ride to see Hardraw Force. It was a magnificent sight with the overnight rain adding to the spectacle, unlike the time in 1986 when celebrating their Sixtieth Wedding Anniversary, I took both of them to see the falls. It was the middle of June and there was little more than a trickle coming over.

There now came a climb that would surely test the OK Supreme. This was the famed Buttertubs Pass that would take us from Wensleydale into Swaledale. The road surface had a great deal of loose gravel and in places was badly rutted, a far cry from the condition that people all over the world saw in 2014, when the first stage of the UK leg of the Tour de France took competitors over the same route.

We set off with a last look across towards Hawes, then began the climb with Dad in first gear for long stretches. As I listened to the exhaust I pondered what Dad may be thinking. The mind of a thirteen year old was recalling the time when I had watched him with the crankcase half on the bench, warming the metal before tapping in the brass bush that had been sent by J.A. Prestwich. (I still have the invoice!). Now here we were with all that happening beneath us, all the parts I had seen turning at unknown revolutions. For long after I puzzled as to how one man can do that then go out and ride long distances with all the stress and strain that is imposed on an engine. It was just another learning curve, because in a few short years I would be performing similar deeds.

At the top of the Pass we stopped to inspect the holes that gave the name to the route, then of course without any warning signs of the danger to the public not to go too close. The 'nanny' state was light years into the future. As he started the engine, I can still recall Dad saying it was all downhill now to West Hartlepool.

Many of the village names we passed through would become familiar in years ahead. Muker, Gunnerside, Healaugh and Reeth, where we stopped for a 'cuppa'. Without wishing to sound too repetitive, this was to be another Dales location that I have returned to many times down the years, sometimes as a base for viewing competitors tackling the famous Scott Trial, or as some might say, infamous. Soon after Leaving Reeth it was noticeable that the hills were becoming smaller and by the time we were entering Richmond and heading for the flat lands that would lead us to Middlesborough, it was top gear all the way.

In Middlesborough we crossed by the Transporter Bridge, riding on a road, as Dad put it. The fare was Threepence, including the 'OK'. We were now within sight of West Hartlepool with just Seaton Carew to pass. This was the sandy beach part of town, although sometimes marred by the outpouring of smoke from the adjacent steel works if the wind was in the wrong direction.

Wednesday was going to be a rest day to give our posteriors a well earned break. We were off to Redcar by train, which the locals considered to be 'posher' than Seaton Carew and without the smoke from the steel works. However, you could be unlucky if the wind was from the west. This time with a smell of all the by-products from I.C.I. Chemicals. Keeping us company were Dad's Brother and Sister, who of course were my Uncle Les and Auntie Marjorie. In the evening the staff at the Gaiety Cinema were joined by two more generations of Mellors'. A truly family business. For me it was another lesson in life as regards to running a cinema business. The first three or four rows were just wooden forms crowded with misbehaved children and only kept in check by the burly doorman who in the daytime worked in the shipyard.

The doorman had said he would show me around the shipyard the next day, so off Dad and I went, catching one of the smart blue and cream trolley buses to the yard entrance. To give an idea of the hard surroundings and certainly not a life I was familiar with, as we were being checked in at the works gate, someone came up to me and said,

"Are you the sucker that's looking for a job." To me this was the language of tough guy film stars like Edward G.Robinson or Humphrey Bogart. But it was an interesting couple of hours. Under repair in the dock were two Royal Navy destroyers and it had puzzled me why we were told that no photographs could be taken when the war had finished two years earlier.

On the Friday night Dad and I were given complimentary tickets to the Empire Theatre. The manager was the brother of Grandfather's business partner so there were always seats available. Being an avid radio listener I knew all the current acts that were doing the rounds. But one newcomer down in the number three spot and certainly meant for stardom, was a very young Max Bygraves. Top of the bill, much to the delight of all the ladies in the audience, was Leslie Hutchinson, otherwise known as 'Hutch' already a radio heartthrob.

The 'OK' had been parked in the yard with only some sacking for protection but came to life easily. Grandmother had insisted on packing sandwiches and they were of course welcome later in the day. Our route was back over the transporter bridge and out towards Saltburn and the coast road down to Whitby. The sandwiches were consumed at Staithes almost under the magnificent railway viaduct that straddled the town and which would disappear in the next decade.

Dad knew a shortcut to avoid Whitby and bring us to the road for Pickering. He did like finding his own 'by-passes and it is one more little mannerism that I have retained. There was only one more steep hill to be climbed. This lay ahead at a spot known as 'The Hole of Horcum' and the Michelin Guide described it as a 1 in 8 ascent with a dangerous turn. The little JAP engine was still performing well and we arrived at the bottom of the hill at the same time as two cycling clubs who were forming a long tailback of riders. There was traffic coming down the hill which limited overtaking and as he tried to pull back to the side he missed selection of first gear, with the result the engine stalled and now being in neutral, needed to be held with both brakes.

With all the cyclists gone he suggested that I walk to the top, as there was little hope of a restart with two-up. As I set off walking, he turned and ran back to the bottom of the hill, starting the engine in gear. It was something I didn't know you could do. Another lesson ticked off. As he passed by I listened to the exhaust note all the way to the top, again in wonderment that you could take these things to pieces, reassemble them and they will continue to do the job they were built for. Plenty to boast about back at school.

After Pickering and Malton, I was back on a familiar road and once past York, I knew it was only around 25 miles to home. In spirit at least, I was game to continue for a good many miles. I was not yet aware that age brought weariness, whereas, my joints and bones were still supple and the mind eager for more, at 46 Dad would not be feeling quite so chirpy. It was one lesson I had yet to tick off the list.

We were now trundling up our cul-de-sac, just seven days since we were going the other way. As we pulled into the drive, the side door opened and there stood Mum. She had arrived home just an hour earlier. It was the end of a perfect week. Dad worked out the mileage to be around 270. His later notes indicated about two pints of oil had been used and he estimated the petrol consumption to have been fifty five miles to the gallon. That 250cc JAP engine with it's minuscule power rating had served us well. As an engine manufacturer I placed them top of my list without even knowing anything about them. In seven years time I would be owning one of their 500cc Speedway engines with a power rating of 55bhp. But all that is for later pages.

In the immediate post war years, many social and industrial Acts were changing or being revised. An important one for workers was to be the annual holidays with pay being increased to two weeks. In the cinema business with all the unsociable hours and varying pay scales, this was a hard won victory. Now with the school summer holiday approaching Dick Hopkins had recently renovated his caravan at Filey. He had sold his Triumph 550cc now that his wife too, had lost the appeal of riding in a sidecar. Still loyal to Triumph though, he had purchased a 250cc Tiger 70 and had asked Dad if he fancied a week at the seaside staying on the site.

Dick's Father was going to drive over, taking the wives and all the luggage, leaving Dad and I and Henry, Dick's son, to travel by motorcycle. I had ridden behind Dick several times before and I soon realised that he wasn't referred to as 'Jovial Dick Hopkins' in the cinema trade for nothing. As he rode along he would be singing all the latest tunes and medleys from film musicals. On the occasions I rode on his pillion I heard most of his repertoire from Al Jolson to Eddie Cantor with a good smattering of the works of Gershwin, Cole Porter and Jerome Kern.

As we were about to start out for Filey on the Saturday, Dick suggested that I rode behind him and Henry behind Dad. By the time we had passed York, he was in full flow with old favourites, plus the hit song of the moment, 'Maybe it's because I'm a Londoner'.

But there was another pleasure waiting for me when we arrived at the caravan park. No more than fifty yards away was the Hull to Scarborough railway line with steam locomotives passing regularly. It was a week to remember.

The summer passed and the sun shone, as it always seemed to do whenever you look back on the time when you were young. Although I made many more local trips on the pillion of the OK Supreme, there were no more long journeys. In fact in late October there was an occurrence that, in description sounds worse than the end result. It was around 4.30pm and Dad was on his way to work. Visibility was not good and his speed was around 20mph and he was riding with side and tail lights lit. Suddenly, a light lorry came out from a left hand turning without warning and although he braked, his shoulder struck the side of the truck and he was thrown to the ground. The machine went across the road into the path of car travelling in the opposite direction and suffered appreciable damage.

As for Dad, he was shaken but unhurt, save for some grazing to the knee and a badly bruised shoulder. Needless to say the offending driver did not stop and was never traced.

The biggest upset was the loss of the OK Supreme as it was beyond any reasonable repair.

I never saw it after the accident which was probably a good thing for it had played such a vital role in my formative years and I'm sure I would have found it upsetting.

These were the days when the Doctor came to your house (how quaint can that be) and Dad was confined to bed to rest and recover from the shock. There was even a District Nurse who called riding a New Hudson auto-cycle, just to check on the bruising. Try getting that service on the National Health today!

For the next six months he was confined to using buses for travelling to and from work, so when he heard that one of the assistant operators was selling his motorcycle to move on to a car and was only asking £5, he called round to see him. The machine was under some corrugated iron sheeting out in a yard and on inspection looked to be complete. Even more convincing was the fact that it started easily despite having been stood for two or three weeks, it was still taxed for the road too.

It was back to BSA for this was a 1936 250cc Model B18 with the registration BRH 387, by coincidence another Hull number, as was the OK Supreme. Once again it was a 4-speed gearbox, but with a hand change control, not that Dad found this a problem. Only forward thinkers like me would regard it as something of an anachronism, but as later pages will reveal, this would be the machine that launched me out onto the roads of north Leeds, although in somewhat illicit circumstances.

A deal was agreed and Dad rode it back to the cinema. Maybe this was a double-edged reason. It was good secure cover while he checked it over and it would give him time to break the news to Mum, who I think by now was tending to put her motorcycling years behind her. The condition was far from pristine. The paintwork was 'tired' and had been touched up in the usual tar brush fashion. Most of the chrome on the tank had gone, but the BSA green was there along with the transfers, including the trademark in that silly place!

His diary shows that very little was spent in repairs, other than a clutch cable, a tail lamp bulb and a gasket, although where for was not specified. When he took it to show his pal, Dick Hopkins, his ever-present joviality came out with, "The shiniest part is the rear chain."

In my later school days I had always shown an aptitude for sport which meant cricket in the summer and rugby (League of course) in the winter. The matches were against other Leeds Schools and were usually played on a Saturday morning, to which Dad would usually take me on the BSA. For one of the last rugby games of the season and close to my April Birthday, I became the toast of the team when they all thought I had ridden to the ground by motorcycle, which shows what can be achieved with a little subterfuge.

The pitch was at the bottom of a slope and higher up the road was a local shop where Dad would usually stop to buy his ten cigarettes for the week. As he was going in I asked, "Alright if I freewheel down to the pitch." He agreed and reminded me to signal a right turn before the entrance. The speed was probably only fifteen miles an hour, but sufficient to carry me past the rest of the team who were busy donning boots and jerseys. As I leaned the BSA against the wall I was surrounded by admirers, every one of them in awe of me with the belief I had ridden here. I even let them go on with their presumption, even after Dad arrived. After all, in those days nobody looked as if they had ridden a motorcycle. He was just standing there in a navy blue overcoat. I was ten feet tall that morning and I also scored two try's.

For the annual holiday in 1948 it was to be my first trip to the Isle of Man for the T.T. Races. This was to continue the appeal of road racing I had first sampled at Scarborough, so much so that I was to return each year until 1954. The first year was in fact the last holiday I had with Dad and Mum, subsequent visits were with school pals, staying at Douglas Holiday Camp, now thankfully boasting chalets, unlike the tents of pre-war years. In 1953 I took the liberty of lowering the camp flag after hearing the sad news of the death of Les Graham. The previous year I had stood within a few feet of him, along with team mate, Bill Doran and a favourite rider from Leeds, Jack Brett. They always say young memories last longer than dreams.

Despite my liking for road racing, I never had any urge to take up the sport and if asked why, I would find it difficult to give a reason. There was to be another form of motorcycle racing which would engage my affection, some may have said to a point of burning ambition. But that is a story for later pages.

I logged more pillion miles with evening trips to the cinema. I still seemed to be on the same rate of two shillings a night for my labours in the operating box. At this period wages or rates of pay played no part in my life and yet I was now less than twelve months away from leaving school. What seemed to be more important was getting to all the local scramble meetings on a Sunday, especially as some of the heroes lived near to me. There were also a good many trials in our area and although it was never my forte, I did acknowledge the skills of the riders and a number of them also rode in national events. I can bring to mind the Ratcliffe Brothers, Geoff Broadbent, Tom Ellis and of course Alan Jefferies, who seemed to be able to turn his hand to any motorcycle sport, always on a Triumph.

As the days began to shorten I now have to own up to my scheme to expand my experience of riding a motorcycle. Cinema opening hours had now been extended to include afternoon shows which often took Dad away by noon. If the weather was fine he would be off on the BSA. Should it be raining then he would take the bus. This meant as darkness came and Mum listening to the radio so as not to miss the latest episode of some mystery thriller, if the weather was fine the BSA would be wheeled out to the next street and I would become just another passing motorcyclist along the gas lit streets of a north Leeds suburb.. How many trips I made or miles covered I really have no idea. The machine had never been fitted with a speedometer so there was no clue to my illicit outings. All I can say it left me wanting more in the years ahead. At the age of fourteen young immature loyalties are often formed for inexplicable reasons, in my case it seemed to be for BSA motorcycles.

Looking back as an octogenarian I have had more BSA machines than any other make. However, I should stress that unlike many riders that it has been my pleasure to know, I have not owned a great many motorcycles. All I have done is kept them for longer periods, nearly forty years in some cases.

There was a period, from the mid sixties into the seventies, when my work in film and television was taking me not only all over this country, but to foreign climes and living in a London flat, where there was not the remotest chance of owning a motorcycle, it was that shabby, well worn little 250cc BSA that I turned to for solace. To be able to return to Leeds and just complete twenty or so miles around the lanes I knew so well was sheer ecstasy. In that well hackneyed song, 'My Way,' there is a line which says, "Regrets, I've had a few." Let me now reveal one of mine.

The fact that I did not keep and restore that BSA for my later years. It would have remained that one link, not only in my motorcycle upbringing, but a link to a man who gave me so much but needed so little in life to be what he loved to call himself, 'the man in the street'. I still miss him very much.

I have perhaps moved on a little too quickly before mentioning the approaching of that significant moment in a teenagers life when he or she leaves school. When suddenly the well-oiled system of education in a relatively strict atmosphere suddenly becomes an adult world of method and management, where waste can not be tolerated, nor time be wasted. During my first week of work, the foreman told me that there were only three ways to do the job. The right way, the wrong way and his way. Work could be a rude awakening for young minds.

With Dad's coaching I had become familiar with everyday tools in the workshop. The correct way to apply an open-ended spanner, which way round a hack saw blade fitted and if you had to use a file without a handle, how to ensure the tang could not damage your hand. He had also taught me the rudiments of electricity and as I was acquiring an interest in cars, an advertisement in the evening paper for an apprenticed auto-electrician seemed to be a suitable opening.

Dad aged 13 and ready to commence work in November 1914. The garden is now the inner courtyard of Leeds Civic Hall and until recent years, there was a tree still in situ from the garden. *(Author)*

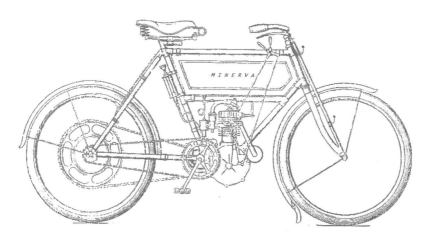

1908 Minerva. Dad's first motorcycle, fitted with a 2-speed gearbox, probably in England. It was given the Leeds Registration number U153.
(From a drawing by Bradley Fraser)

Dad's 1914 Blackburne motorcycle, nick named 'Nellie', the beautiful Blackburne
Model. The reason is related in the text. *(Author)*

LIST OF COMPETITORS

Number and Name	Make	H.P.	Reg. No.	Driver	Theatre or Firm
1 Brooks, O.	Brooks'JAP	8	U.I.	Self	Headingley P. H.
2 Goodal, Percy	G. N.	8.7	HD 1267	Self	Macclesfield P.Pal.
3 Pattison, J.	Calthorpe	2 ½	X 8590	Self	Neville Bruce Ltd.
4 Harrison, P	Moon	25/30	KB 4252	A.Dewis	F. Lasky
5 Stone, G.	Overland	19	U 9658	Self	F. Bo
6 Kemp, C	G.N	8/10	U 8347	Self	F.P.L Film Serv.
7 Whiteley,J.R.	Belsize-Brad.	9	NW 472	Self	Vitagraph
8 Barker, Benj.	Jowett	7	AK 5769	Self	Vitagraph
9. Marshall, H. S.	Metro- Tyler	2¾	U 5101	Self	Wardour Films
10 Knapton, G. W.	Enfield-Allday	10	-----	Self	Butcher's
11 Hopkins, H.	L.M.C.	6	AK 5769	Self	People's' Palace
12 Leach, F. C.	Alvis	10	HP 2479	Self	Pearl
13 Agnew, E. C.	F.I.A.T.	15	U 1959	Self	Gaumont
14 Green, T. H.	Calthorpe	10.4	C 2419	Self	Wellington F. Ser.
15 Jay, W.	Rover	8	NW 2098	Self	Fox Film Co. Ltd.
16 Buckler, J.	Triumph	4	U 8907	Self	Carlton Cinema
17 Mellor, T.	Blackburne	3½	U 3941	Self	Tower Picture Ho.
18 Coulthard, H.	Rover	8	U 7627	Self	General
19 Hanbury, R.	Ford	20	U 7266	Self	Stoll
20 Butler, H.	Kingsbury,Jr.	8.9	WR 4816	Self	Queen's H.,Lstrdyk.
21 Camp, A. J.	Sunbeam	3½	C 2449	Self	Crown P.H. Cstlfrd..
22 Brooks, W. R.	Blackburne	2¾	U 484	Self	Headingley Pic. Ho.
23 Tidswell, J.F.	Vauxhall	25	------	Self	Tower Picture Ho.
24 Hodgkinson, J.E.	Enfield	8	WY 199	Self	Pic. Ho. Tadcaster
25 Fountain, Geo.	Ford	20	U 9018	Self	Kilner's
26 Loyde, W. W.	Rover	8	AJ 6537	Self	Rialto P. P. Hull
27 Sunderland, F.	Calcott	10	--------	Self	N. C. P. Ltd.
28 Parker, F.	Rover	8	--------	Self	Colliseum, Leeds
29 Wincup, C. H.	James	2¼	U 3161	Self	Wincup
30 Wincup, C. H.	Mayflower	20	XH 6393	Self	Wincup
31 Pemberton, John.	Norton	4	--------	Self	Pav., Hunslet,Leeds
32 Phillips, Wm.	Star	10/12	--------	Self	I.A.P Co. Bdfrd.
33 Anderton, E.	Vauxhall	25	---------	Self	Grand P. H. Bdfrd.
34 Roberts, G.	Ford	---		Self	
35 Woffinden, J. J.	Singer	10	WR 4667	Self	Oxford, Mexborough
36 Thornton, T	Wolseley	16/20	AK 2781	Self	Oak Lane,Bradford

Programme from a 1922 hill climb at Eccup near Leeds. Not only is it a 'who's who' of
the Yorkshire cinema trade in the 1920s, but the registration numbers would now be
worth a fortune. *(Author)*

U1 was the first motorcycle to be registered in Leeds. It was built by Owen Brooks, a local cinema owner, using available parts based around a JAP engine. It featured in hill climbs around the Leeds area until the 1922 legislation prohibiting pace making and speed events on public roads was passed by Parliament. The photograph was taken outside the former stables at the rear of the Cottage Road Cinema (originally the Headingley Picture House) Leeds and although the cinema is still standing, the lovely old stone workshops have been demolished. *(Courtesy of VMCC Library)*

Model T Ford. The type of car owned by Grandfather Mellor and maintained by Dad as a teenager. *(M. Sanderson)*

Dad's first and only car, 1908 Clement Talbot. The 175th Leeds registration number may now be featured on some Bentley or Porsche. *(Author)*

1921 and Dad and Mum are officially 'walking out' together. They had a day trip to Scarborough and had this picture taken in a studio. *(Author)*

1925, 350cc AJS as found in an outhouse and ridden home. In the 1920s if it was not raining, it seems you dressed casually for motorcycling! *(Author)*

Governor's Bridge in 1927. Dressed normally for a lap of the TT course!

Leader board at the 1927 Senior TT races. No 38 Alec Bennett had slowly worked his way to 1st place. The lady in the cloche hat is mum, smiling for the camera. *(Author)*

Mum and Champion Queno von Brunanhoff, otherwise known as Que. I was raised on stories about the tricks he could perform. *(Author)*

Customers' own machines driven at owners' risk and responsibility.   Telephone **52540**.

DR. TO

Harold Barrett

Motor Cycle Exchange Specialist

Terms arranged to
s u i t   individual
requirements.

Service and Works at

SPOT GARAGE, HIGHBURY LANE
MONKBRIDGE ROAD, MEANWOOD
(NEAR CAPITOL)

Insurance Claims,
complete overhauls
and repairs, etc.

———— L E E D S ————

M N   S. Mellor   3/5/32.
        14 Wyke Beck View Leeds 19

£o.

1. Sports Sidecar
(fitted to AJS. Solo.)   £5 . 0 . 0.

less deposit.   £ 1 . 0 . 0

£ 4 . 0 . 0

1932 prices during the recession. Some would say the pound was worth more then.
(Author)

67

1935 BSA Blue Star before the sidecar was fitted. It was the 350cc model and once again Dad had economy in mind, even though his boss was paying for it.
(Dealers Photograph)

BSA Sports Sidecar fitted to the 1935 Blue Star. It was in this sidecar that I began my motorcycling apprenticeship upon mum's knee. *(Dealers photograph)*

Then I came along. My fascination with steam locomotives began at an early age. Should anyone be interested, the locomotive is one of Mr Gresley's 'Hunt' Class. 'The Grafton' at Neville Hill Shed, Leeds. *(Author)*

My fascination with wheels began at an early age too! Before school even. *(Author)*

Bob Wilson was one of my heroes when I was 16. He was Yorkshire Hill Climb Champion in 1950, riding a machine powered by a JAP speedway engine. This was at Douglas Holiday Camp during TT week and he had no objection to posing with some young upstart who kept babbling on about JAP engines. *(Author)*

16 and downhearted having just failed my first driving test for looking down while operating the hand gear change. It was the start of happy memories of this little BSA and how I wish I had retained it for future restoration. *(Author)*

The dreams of a sixteen year old grass track enthusiast. A 1928 350cc JAP engine in a Panther frame. It did run, briefly, as related in the text. *(Author)*

Assembled by Eric Langton to make a typical Yorkshire grass track machine. The front engine plates are not only lightened, but stepped to move the engine to the left. *(Author)*.

My Fan Club sometimes totalled as many as 2 members! One fan letter said, "If you are not the brightest thing to hit the British Speedway scene, then I'm a Dutchman. It was signed, Hans Van Gelderhoffen! *(Author)*

Pals for life from the age of 13. Dick Hopkins (left) and Dad at Dick's caravan at Filey. Dick's father's 1932 Standard in the background. One of my many teachings was, you were not dressed without a tie, even on holiday. *(Author)*

Dad and Mum appearing as extras in a BBC Look North programme about old cinemas. They were queuing to go in. *(Author)*

My grey porridge work horse during my early RAF years. Dad enjoyed it too, having no problem adapting between foot and hand gear change. In the background is the 16'x8' garage we built from angle iron and asbestos sheets. *(Author)*

My 1951 BSA alloy engine B32 which served as transport to the RAF camp and Dales grass tracks. Dad had just returned from a trip to the shops, such was his casual approach to motorcycling in 1954.

Trying to broadside a BSA B32 was nigh impossible. Changing to a JAP powered machine in a suitable frame made a big difference. This is one of the meetings while I was serving in the RAF. *(Author)*

The start of my penchant for BSA M20s. DXF 446 was registered in London in 1937, the first year of the M20. The stud below the tank transfer shows it was supplied with hand gear change. At some time after the war, both engine and gearbox were changed. 4 bolts removed the child/adult body and a platform carried my grass track machine. *(Author)*

This is the 500cc JAP speedway engine, which provided a great deal of the story content of the book. In standard form it had a compression ratio of 14 to 1. This was later increased to 16 to 1 with re-designed cams.

Eric Langton with an experimental Norton speedway machine. Belle Vue pits did not change from this early 1930s view, to me arriving in 1956. *(Author)*

FOUR TYPES OF SPEEDWAY FRAME MANUFACTURED

JAP ENGINES FROM STOCK

Eric K. Langton

SPEEDWAY SPECIALIST

ODSAL STADIUM
BRADFORD

SPECIALLOID
PISTONS

Phone No. 22981

"CLOMARD" LINERS
FITTED

Eric was not only a fine engineer, but a shrewd businessman too, as portrayed in his card. I have always regretted not getting to know him better, but he still made a big impression on one hesitant young lad from Leeds. *(Author)*

I remember very little about the interview, but I must have appeared as a suitable applicant, maybe because I was wearing a tie. Another of Dad's teachings. The logic being that it gave you an air of authority. Whatever the reason, I was asked to start the following Monday, one month after my fifteenth birthday. It would be a 44 hour week, including Saturday morning, not unusual for the time and the weekly wage would be 22 shillings, rising to 30 shillings after a six month probationary period. That would now be £1.50.

I was now one of the working class. The daily routine would start at the bus queue. Same faces, same conversation and same seat on the bus with a repeat performance at 5.30pm. I could change the formula in fine weather by cycling to work, but there was a tough climb on the homeward journey.

The work itself, after an initial settling in period, mainly involved stripping vehicle electrical units for the senior staff to recondition. These would be starter motors, dynamos, windscreen wiper motors, Magnetos, both car and motorcycle, including the infamous Maglita, that wonderful invention based on the 'something for nothing' principle and fuel pumps, both the electrical SU type and the AC mechanical unit.

I was of course at the bottom of the pecking order and looked up to everyone else. Then, as is the way with human behavior, two more apprentices started and I was looked up to. After six months I was trusted to reassemble fuel pumps and wiper motors.

Most of the crowd from school had found work within the motor trade, either as mechanics or in panel beating. One Saturday, someone mentioned they were going to see speedway racing at Odsal Stadium, Bradford and if I was interested, they would be catching the Bradford bus at a given time. However, it did mean that in order to catch the last bus back, we would have to leave before the end of racing. It was to be a bus ride that changed my life.

That Saturday night in September, 1949, from the moment I saw the first race, I knew this was what I wanted to do. By the time I was catching the bus back to Leeds my ambition was to be a speedway rider. But it was not to happen overnight, nor was it a rags to riches tale.

But how does a fifteen year old apprentice from Leeds become a speedway rider? Perhaps at this point of the story I should introduce two names of Yorkshire motorcyclists, who we have already met in earlier years. These were the Langton Brothers, Oliver, who was born in 1906 and Eric,born in 1909. They were Yorkshire through and through. I say that after I was once in a conversation with road racing personality, Dennis Parkinson, who summed up the Langton's with, "Yorkshire goes through them like Blackpool goes through rock." I had been raised on stories of their dare devil stunts when dirt track racing (the original name for speedway) first came to Leeds in 1928.

It will be recalled that we have already met Oliver and his penchant for befriending motorcycling cinema operators to obtain complimentary tickets. But as motorcyclists they were a force to be reckoned with in competitive events. A brief run down may give an idea.

They both won Gold Medals in the London to Edinburgh Trial in the early twenties. They competed in the T.T. Oliver won the Scott Trial in 1927; Eric won it in 1928; Then when dirt track racing arrived they were both nigh unbeatable. They both became members of the all-conquering Belle Vue team of the 1930s. Although Oliver retired in 1934, Eric was to continue riding until 1946.

It may seem I am over stressing the careers of these two men, but they were both brilliant engineers and played a large part in my first faltering steps into competitive motorcycling. Just one more example of Eric's ability. He once told me that in the same year as he won the Scott Trial, he also won the Southern Scott. He was riding to the meeting and following his Father's car along the Great North Road when he hit a pot hole and collapsed the rear wheel rim. His Father drove into Grantham to buy a spare rim and Eric rebuilt the wheel at the side of the road.

Dad had said that Oliver could often be found on a Saturday morning at the family building business in the centre of Leeds. It would mean asking if I could leave work perhaps half an hour early and I estimated it would take ten minutes to cycle there. When I arrived, Oliver was in the yard with his head under the bonnet of an old Riley saloon. The modern equivalent of what I was about to do would be, if some Italian street urchin went up to Valantino Rossi and said, "How do I become a road racer."

He looked up and I spoke first. I told him who I was and that my Father was Chief Operator at the Strand Cinema and, bye the way, "Could he tell me how to become a speedway rider."

If he was amused, it didn't show and there seemed to be an eternity of silence before he said, "You need to speak to my Brother." Then he returned to what he was doing under the bonnet.

I was on the point of turning to leave, when his head again came from under the bonnet and he said, "Come back in an hour and I'll take you."

That was a long hour. Luckily, not too far away were the two principle motorcycle dealers in the town. B.J. Jenkins, who was the Triumph and Ariel agent and Watson Cairns who were BSA and Norton. They stood almost opposite one another and anyone who was watching me would have been puzzled by my constant crossing and recrossing between the two for almost an hour.

As we drove out of the yard, I had no idea where Eric lived and did not have the courage to ask. Oliver opened the conversation by asking where I worked. When I told him he laughed and asked, "Do you think they would have a set of dynamo brushes for this model?" Then he pointed to the ammeter and added, "That's why it isn't charging."

"Won't the battery go flat?" I asked nervously.

"No, I stuck a magneto on as a temporary measure." He replied.

I could only marvel at such ingenuity. Not wanting to appear a young upstart full of inane chatter the only other conversation was about Dad's current motorcycle and the loss of the OK Supreme.

By now I had realised we were heading for Bradford and I soon recognised Odsal Stadium. We stopped outside a workshop and I followed him inside. Eric was engaged in welding tubes together and I could see this was forming one of his renowned frames. He briefly stopped, raised his goggles and looked across at me. Oliver told him, "He wants to know how to become a speedway rider."

Eric lowered his goggles and continued welding. If Oliver was a man of few words, Eric was even less. Oliver busied himself around the workshop while I stood and watched Eric at work until he finally lifted his goggles and said, "Can you ride a bike?"

I assured him I could. "Then get yourself a JAP engine and go grass track racing." He added. And that was the end of the advice.

Oliver had loaded some equipment into the Riley and was ready to go. Very little was said on the return journey. He asked if I knew about Kidsons. This was the place where all impecunious motorcyclists went for spares. At this period new parts were not readily available so it was a case of replacing a worn out part with one which was not so worn out! Every town in Britain must have had such an emporium during and after the austere post war years.

After six months my wage increased to thirty shillings. £1.50 in modern terms and I thought I was well off! My first solo visit to Kidsons, I had been with Dad before, found them breaking an early thirties 250cc Panther and I could have everything except the engine for £5. I could leave a deposit of £1 and hoped to raise the balance. Having told them my plan, it was agreed that if I did not want to use the heavy mudguards, they would reduce the price of a JAP engine they had for sale. This was a 1928 350cc complete with carburettor and magneto. I was up and running. Well up at least!

With my copy of 'Tuning for Speed' to hand, I set out to convert the engine to run on Methanol. The text had said you could raise the compression by removing metal from the cylinder head or barrel. How much was not specified, so I just asked my local garage to remove some.

Throughout the winter months the project slowly developed. Dad and I had replaced the shed with a car sized garage which provided an ideal workplace to assemble the 'Thing'. The name by which Mum referred to it.

1950 was the year I had been waiting for. My sixteenth Birthday. It may also have been the year Mum was dreading, but there was no outward objections raised to my application for a Provisional Licence. I placed a 'Motorcycle Wanted' advertisement in our local evening paper, suitably worded to indicate a beginner with a limited income. The first phone call asked if I could afford £10. If so he had a 1936 Model 50 350cc Norton for sale.

The next day was Sunday and Dad and I went along to see the Norton. It was a runner, had been stored away during the war and everything still worked The owner had even scrounged half a gallon of petrol to ensure it still started. It would mean raiding my savings for the grass track project and Dad using his last petrol coupon of the month, so I paid the £10 and we rode it home. Dad was impressed with the general all round performance and thought I had got a bargain. The only apparent fault was it did not indicate a charge on the ammeter.

All the necessary application papers for licence, insurance and change of ownership were completed and the big day arrived for my first fully legal ride! Memory can be a perplexing mental power for as I have indicated earlier, I do tend to have an astute mind when recalling the past. Yet that day when I rode out displaying 'learner plates' is totally erased. All I know is it did happen!

26 May, 1950, was ' a red letter' day for all road users in Britain. It signalled the end of petrol rationing. Newspapers had full front page photographs of people celebrating by burning coupons and decorating petrol pumps. Ten years of virtually no petrol brought massive traffic jams around the country. But there was a' sting in the tail ' for a week later the price of a gallon was increased to three shillings (15p), the highest it had been since 1920.

My Driving Test was booked for the end of June, however, on the morning of the test, I discovered a rear wheel puncture in the Norton and had to resort to the 250cc BSA. All seemed to be going well until the Instructor advised me I had failed due to looking down while operating the hand gear change. A month later I was making a second attempt on the Norton and passed with the same Instructor too.

I now had the freedom of the open road. But first I had to finish the 'Thing'. I had tried pulling the rear wheel over compression and there was every indication that it would start, which was encouraging, so I sent off an entry form for a local grass track meeting. I was now also a member of West Leeds Motorcycle Club.

I had total family support at that first event. Mum and Dad of course and Brother Ron and his current girl friend. Sadly I am unable to relate a story of success for my debut. While preparing for practice the engine was started, which was a thrill in itself. It appeared to respond to the throttle too. But after about five minutes it could no longer suffer in silence and with a noise best described as somewhere between a bang and a thud, the whole cylinder barrel and head moved upwards, stripping the four base nuts from their studs. I was going to be a non-starter.

Amazingly, there seemed to be no other serious damage and I was able to remove the engine. A few days later I turned up at Eric Langton's workshop and asked if anything could be done to rectify the problem. It was sometime before he spoke, then he finally exhaled and said, "When I told you to get yourself a JAP engine I meant a Speedway engine." There were several around the workshop in varying stages of repair to illustrate his point. I then went on to tell him that I had raised the compression on the vintage engine.

"Leave it with me and I'll make you some new studs and I'll have a look round for an a engine." That was the longest sentence he had spoken to me.

About three weeks later, Eric rang me to say he had rebuilt the engine so off I went on the Norton to collect it. He had made new studs with longer nuts that could be tightened to a much greater tension than previously. He had also gone to the trouble of measuring the compression ratio and found this to be close to 10 to 1, when in reality, it should be 4 to 1. He had reduced the ratio and suggested I use petrol in future.

There was another meeting coming up, this was billed as a 'mountain grass track,' which was usually a tactful way of describing a rough track. I was too late to get a programme entry, but the Secretary said if I turned up I could be a late entry.

I actually did some practice laps and even though it was the only machine entered with girder forks and it wasn't a perfect oval track, I felt a tingle of excitement that would return again and again in the years ahead. What I was not yet conversant with were such technical matters as gear ratios, mixture settings and tyre pressures. I was also at a disadvantage by having no positive stop gear change. The original had of course been a hand change machine. But I lined up in my first heat and did not disgrace myself, unlike one rider who stalled on the line, a second one who's machine began to smoke badly within a few yards and another who collided at the first bend and fell. What let me down was the rear tyre creeping and pulling the valve from the inner tube. I didn't know about security bolts either.

Riding at the meeting on a machine fitted with speedway JAP engine, was a man later to be come a good friend and, in my eyes at least, a hero. This was Walt Rathmell, who could best be described as one of nature's gentlemen. He was the type of person who found time to speak to a sixteen year old novice and sympathise with someone who was trying to make a mark in life. Walt began telling me about the grass track meetings in the Dales, usually associated with an agricultural show, and where girder forks would not be a subject of derision. He recommended me to join the Craven Motorcycle Club for more information. It was certainly a step in the right direction.

I called to see Eric Langton and showed him a photograph of the 'Thing,' adding that it now ran but without much power. Without much enthusiasm, he just said, "I'm not surprised, you would do better on the Norton."

There was the germ of an idea. Strip everything off that wasn't required, fit alloy guards and knobbly tyres and maybe I would do better. This was my winter project, in addition to writing to speedway managers asking for the prospects of a trial. Out of nearly twenty, two replied asking if I had my own machine. Eric told me to stay with grass track racing for now.

The weekly speedway magazines were bemoaning the fact that attendances at most meetings were falling, whereas, five years earlier they had been equal to football crowds. The Editors were asking for reasons. There didn't seem to be any. But my ambition was unchanged and for now it was, as the Americans would say, 'put on the back-burner.'

Converting the Norton was not difficult and without all the accoutrements it looked quite sporty. Dad didn't see it that way and Mum couldn't see the point, but it could serve two uses. A grass track meeting and a means of transport. For this I was introduced to that eccentric term so beloved by trials riders of the fifties. The Bobby Dodger! These were a simple set of cycle lamps attached front and rear and so making night time riding perfectly legal.

It became an essential part of your tool bag when riding at a show meeting in the Dales. The grass track racing was usually the final part of the programme and would sometimes not commence until after 6pm. Taking part in some of these meetings occasionally did mean a little deception had to be used to have an afternoon off work.

Easter, 1951 was one time when I was 'attending an old aunt's funeral.' Walt Rathmell was entered which gave me an immediate contact. This led to a meeting with Eric Carr, who was the son of Jack Carr, a well-known motorcyclist in the twenties and who Dad had seen at hill climbs. Another rider I came to have a high regard for was Peter Lloyd who was six years my senior and had begun riding speedway at sixteen. Peter had ridden for a number of teams, but was now feeling the effect of the decline and had turned to grass track racing. With some success I might add.

The Norton ran well but was totally outclassed by the JAP engines fitted to many of the competitors machines. But I joined in with the also rans and was to become an accepted member amongst the likes of Ken Jones with a Velocette, Dick Harling and Bob Middleton who had machines fitted with the 350cc version of the JAP ; referred to as the

Grass Track engine. Bob was a lovely Dales character, again with time for a youngster and I was to learn in later years, that he was an uncle of Bill Wilkinson from Kettlewell.

By and large it was a good season for me. No success as far as winning races, but just becoming a part of the scene. In June there was the holiday in the Isle of Man with Geoff Duke winning the Senior Race for the second time. Back home the grass track season finished with three Dales show meetings and my first prize money, only £1 but a great morale booster at least. Another seventy four and I could afford to buy a JAP engine.

By chance I met Eric at a Bradford speedway meeting. He looked after all the engine tuning for the team. I told him about taking his advice and converting the Norton for grass track but I was still saving towards a speedway engine. He came out with a profound statement that had never occurred to me. In another six months I would be called up for National Service and any chance of racing would have to be postponed.

Just after my eighteenth Birthday I received the 'Calling Up' papers along with a date for a medical. I entered for the first grass track of the season, which was around a sports field and very smooth. Needless to say those with a JAP engine were in their element, while I and my equals vied for the lower places. What the future held I had no idea. Mum was fretting as the daily news concerned the Korean War and British troops of all three services were being sent out. I took the decision to sell the Norton. A mechanic at one of the town's motorcycle dealers took a fancy to it as a quirky hack.

Fate can be a strange bedfellow. When I attended the Registration Office where all three services were based, I was of the belief that it would be the compulsory two years in the Army then back to civvy street. When I entered the office there was no one to be seen. Perhaps it was his tea break or he may have gone along the corridor to the toilet. So I went up one flight of stairs to the RAF office.

This was attended with a genial looking officer and a smart looking Corporal. I was invited to sit, which struck me as a good start. Was I looking forward to National Service? My reply about doing it because I had no choice brought an immediate reply. Had I considered the options? He then went on to explain that by serving an extra twelve months brought a number of benefits not available to anyone serving two years. He listed such things as, twice as much leave, double pay, higher clothing allowance and paid reserve for four years, along with a uniform maintenance payment. There was also a bigger selection of trades available.

It was very tempting and twelve months didn't seem too long so I signed on the dotted line. Back home when I announced what I had done, Mum took it as if I had signed on for twelve years in the Foreign Legion. But unbeknown then the final outcome was very satisfying. I went off to a tearful family farewell to begin basic training followed by trade training for which I had chosen, Engine Mechanic (Turbine). At the end of the course as the names came up for permanent postings all the overseas names came up. Cyprus, Singapore, Germany. I followed the names alphabetically to mine. RAF Leeming. That had a familiar sound to it. Then I found it on the map. It was sited on the Great North Road, six miles south of Catterick and only forty miles from home. I was to spend the next 2 ½ years there.

The station was home to a squadron of Meteor NF11s which was the 2-seat night fighter version, this meant there were a lot of night flying exercises. Once I had settled in I volunteered for night flying duties on a more or less permanent basis. The big advantage was if it was cancelled for inclement weather around 9pm; on a Friday evening you were free until Monday morning. My next move was to buy another motorcycle.

Dad found a neighbour who was selling a 1945 BSA 250cc C10 side vale model. Pure grey porridge in many eyes but it was cheap, reliable and very economical. The one fault was it did not like the long stretch of the Great North Road and would run out of puff about 40mph.

Early in 1953 I saw an advertisement in the Leeds paper for a BSA B32 350cc with all alloy engine. My plan was two-fold. It would be my weekend transport but as I was near to Wensleydale and Swaledale, I would be able to enter for some show meetings too. In 1953 I rode at three events, while in 1954 I made it to four. Those that started around 6pm were ideal, because in high summer, night flying did not commence until at least 10pm. They were happy years at Leeming and having thirty days leave each year I was able to continue with my visits to the T.T. Races. I often thought about the Army Recruiting officer who was missing from his office. Where might I have been sent had he been there?

My weekly copy of Speedway Star continued to give a gloomy outlook for the sport. More tracks were closing, some in mid-season before completing all their fixtures. My ambition was still simmering on the back burner!

Early in 1954 I called to see Eric Langton. Once again it seemed fate had chosen this day for my visit. He asked me if I was still interested in a speedway engine. Of course I was. He told me about an engine he had supplied to a rider in Birmingham, having received half payment, with the rest to be paid in two months. It seems he had welshed on the agreement (not the sort of thing you do to a Yorkshireman) and Eric said he had 'sent in the heavy mob' to recover it. I dare not ask what that meant but agreed to buy it. He asked what I was going to put it in, then added, "Come and have a look at this." We went to the backyard where he uncovered what had been an Ariel military model. He had sold the engine but the rest remained complete. "Just the thing for the tracks you ride." he said.

Next weekend there was a message from him. He now had the engine which was complete and in good order. I was now the owner of a speedway JAP engine. Which at the time was the most powerful single cylinder unsupercharged engine in the world. It was another step in the right direction.

It was agreed that I would take on some of the basic work, such as the gearbox, clutch, wheel hubs and arrange to have speedway sized rims fitted. Eric would make the engine plates and shorten the wheelbase by modifying the forks and supply any ancillary parts. By the end of the year it was looking like a Yorkshire grass track machine.

Unlike grass track racing in most other parts of England, Yorkshire grass tracks were insular and somewhat unique, perhaps parochial. We had not followed the trend for rear suspension, gear boxes and telescopic front forks. Girder forks and rigid frames still ruled. This was certainly the scene at many of the Dales shows and though there were those who wished to bestow the term 'flat earth' upon us, most of us had no desire to change. It was pure motor sport for our enjoyment and that of others. Perhaps we looked upon it as the 'poor man's style of speedway racing.

Before I took the machine away from his workshop, Eric told me some news that came as a shock. He had decided to sell up and move out to Perth in West Australia. Sadly, due to a change in his sailing dates, I was not able to bid him farewell and thank him for everything he had done to help me. He was one of those people that pass in and out of our lives and yet leave a lasting impression that is never forgotten. One very poignant moment I discovered after he had died in 2001 aged 93. His Grandchildren came back to scatter his ashes on the family grave at Pudsey, between Leeds and Bradford. The cemetery was less than a mile from the field where I had ridden my first grass track bike and where the cylinder had burst upwards.

In January,1955, with five months of service left, I began to think about transport for the new JAP. Riding to meetings was now not possible, unless of course you lived in some remote part of the Yorkshire Dales, but that is another story! I was told of someone who was selling a BSA combination and rang him. The model was the M20 fitted with a child/adult sidecar, easily detachable and replaced with a wooden platform. It dated from 1937, the first year of production, however, it had been updated with a later WD engine and gearbox, originally having been hand change. It proved to be a very robust and reliable outfit and was to endear me to the M20 from then on.

At last I could give the JAP a test run and set off to a remote and now disused airfield, near York. It started very easily despite the standard compression of 14 to 1. I ensured the engine was warm before engaging a gear and opening the throttle. It was to be one of those heart stopping moments. The acceleration was unbelievable as the steering became so light due to the front wheel wanting to lift. I still have a vivid recall to this day.

The first meeting of the year was at Cowthorpe, near Wetherby. The field could only be described as 'undulating', a word popularised by Dennis Parkinson in later years when commentating at televised scrambles. How to control the power available was going to be a steep learning curve, so Dad marked the programme heats as, 5th, fell, 4th and last due to a puncture. I still had not yet mastered security bolts.

For the next two or three meetings, I went along as a spectator. What was I doing wrong? At a meeting near Skipton I was able to be mechanic to Walt Rathmell and to listen and learn from him. He suggested maybe I was trying too hard, adding that eagerness was one thing and that it was the end result that counted. He was a wise old owl and much revered in Yorkshire grass track circles. It was a great tragedy to our sport when he was injured in an industrial accident, resulting in the loss of his sight.

For the August Bank Holiday there were meetings on consecutive days. Monday was back at Cowthorpe where Dad marked the programme with a string of third and fourth places, but just outside the prize money.

Next day, Tuesday, was still a holiday in the north of England at that time. The track was at Clifton Park, Rotherham and was packed with people. These meetings had begun at the end of the war as part of a 'Holidays at Home' campaign and were still popular. I note from the programme that also riding was a dear friend from Leeds, who, like me, was committed to Yorkshire grass track style. This was Dave Giles, with whom I still talk to regularly even though he is some four thousand miles away in Canada.

Our friendship went back to the forties when we tried to emulate our speedway heroes with cycle speedway. David's Father was the local Vicar and had allowed him to build a track in the rear garden of the vicarage. This was complete with lights, pits and a starting gate with tapes. David had recently discarded his BSA B32 machine for a speedway JAP and this may have been his first outing.

The track at Clifton Park was the perfect setting and an ideal oval with a natural banking to accommodate the crowds. Racing was on a points system and I ended the meeting with five points at five shillings a point. This included a second place behind Sid Mintey, a wily old fox from early post war racing.

On the following Saturday, there was yet another meeting and I improved upon my points tally. Once again the crowd was huge. So much so that in later years at Bank Holiday it became the practice to hold an afternoon meeting and repeat the racing in the evening to accommodate all the people.

Later in the month a number of Dales shows were held. At Malham and Trawden I was able to feature in the results and at least covered my entry and fuel costs. To round of 1955 I entered for a meeting at Wigan. This was new ground and I was to be rubbing shoulders, literally in some races, with new names. The Terratta Brothers had long been Cheshire and Welsh title holders, along with Andy Courtney from Southport. As I was to learn on a number of occasions, Andy would test your nerve by leaning on you in the bend. Depending on how brave you were, you either closed the throttle or held it open!

1956 was not the best of seasons. Races were lost due to trivial faults, possibly through shoddy maintenance. Clutch and gearbox problems, then a spate of punctures made me realise that if you want to get ahead, attention to detail was first and foremost.

There was a change of transport for 1957. The M20 had given sterling service but had it's limitations. I was wanting to travel further, possibly with two machines if a colleague wished to join me. The pick-up truck was becoming fashionable amongst riders and I found the Standard 10hp would suit my needs, being economical and able to carry a second machine. As Dad was still happy with the little 250cc BSA; I advertised the sidecar outfit and had no problem in finding an immediate buyer.

The traditional Easter Monday meeting had now moved to Esholt near Bradford and was to prove the break I had been waiting for. Dave Giles and I were out in the first heat and both had a good start in front of local favourite, Maurice Wilkinson. Maurice was a good rider, but of the sprung frame, gearbox and feet up variety. He hated anything with girder forks. "They ride under your elbows." was one of his complaints. As we came into the first bend, a photographer from the Yorkshire Post was looking for something depicting holiday sport and he caught it by having the first four riders out of ten in his viewfinder.

The Editor must have liked it for it appeared on the front page of the Yorkshire Evening Post the same evening. Even more opportune, it was seen by Oliver Langton who got in touch with an offer I had been waiting seven years for. I had seen little of him over the years, an odd occasion at Eric's workshop, where I can only presume that he knew about the grass track machine Eric had built for me. But more important, Oliver was in charge of the training school at Belle Vue Speedway and always on the lookout for new talent, despite the depressed state of British Speedway.

He suggested that if I could put a suitable machine together, he would arrange for me to attend the Monday afternoon and evening sessions. Eric had given me the 'bare bones' of a speedway frame when he was clearing his workshop and as it was complete with the countershaft and clutch, I was well on the way. It would of course mean using my engine and I was to become very proficient in changing this from one to the other. Often working after midnight if I had been riding on the Sunday and wanted to attend on a Monday. All of which still revolved around working as an auto electrician.

I was fortunate in being able to obtain many parts from Oliver, who it seems had cleared the residue after Eric emigrated and by May I had a complete machine ready, except for the engine change. Dave Giles and I had decided to try pastures new and entered for a meeting near Boston in

Lincolnshire. It would be a busy weekend because we were also entered for a show meeting at Clapham on Saturday evening.

I spoke to Oliver and told him the particular Monday I was hoping to attend and would he arrange the necessary gate passes. I tried to plan the engine change so that apart from the complete engine, there would be nothing else to transfer. The first attempt took around two hours, but it did improve after the third or fourth change.

In the meantime, our trip to Boston was not without it's problems. The track was a 1000 yards and fairly rough, whereas Yorkshire tracks were rarely no more than 440 yards. We were both totally outclassed by the likes of Arthur Stuffins, Jackie Sewell and Don Nourish. But revenge was mine a season later when we were all racing at Clifton Park, Rotherham with it's tiny oval track. I finished the meeting by winning the 'Flying Twelve' and taking home 2 weeks wages. It was a case of 'horses for courses.'

As I drove into the Belle Vue complex in Hyde Road, Manchester I was seeing everything from a different viewpoint. I had attended as a spectator many times but in the grandstand. To drive in took you under and behind the whole operation of rides, stalls and amusement arcades until you arrived at the pits. Once you had wheeled your machine in the whole picture became clear..

The trip from Leeds had taken longer than expected and this was of course long before Motorways. The road over the Pennines from Huddersfield was tedious with the slowest lorry setting the pace. It meant that there was only an hour of practice left and little time to prepare. But there were willing hands to start and warm the engine while I did a quick change.

I was instructed to just do a number of circulating laps to begin. The reason being, the track had not yet been prepared after the last meeting on Saturday night and the surface was not even. To me after some of the grass tracks I had ridden on it looked perfect. Eventually, I was waved down and told to go to the starting line. As the tapes were not working I could make a start in my own time.

This was it. It was my moment of truth. Either I would make an impression or fall flat on my face. I did neither! The first bend seem to come up very quickly and the front wheel wanted to slide first. As I eased the throttle off there was a tendency to drift out towards the fence and the wooden boards did not look to have any cushioning effect.

I returned to the pits gate. The track marshal knew the problem and shouted 'when you feel you are losing the front wheel, open out.' He then signalled me to follow the rider in front, adding,' when he does it, you do it.' Next time was better and the next lap was even better. It was having the nerve to open the throttle when you feel you are losing the machine and going to fall flat on your ear. I realised that there was no comparison to cornering on grass. The reaction of the tyres were never going to be equal on the two differing surfaces. By the time I had done another five or six laps and just before the 'end of session' light was shown, I was feeling, I'm not sure what I was feeling. Confident maybe or just overawed by the whole occasion. Maybe there was just a hint of satisfaction.

Back at the pits gate as I took my helmet off, the marshal came up and said, "It makes a big difference when you open the throttle, all we have to do now is speed you up a bit."

As I drove back to Leeds I was almost wild with excitement as I tried to relive each Lap. I was already telling myself, next time I must do this, or next time I won't do that. Whatever I was feeling, if I could have bottled it I would have made my fortune.

Believing in yourself is probably the best way to overcome any inhibitions and to rid yourself of any reticence you just have to go out and do it. You convince other people and, more importantly, you convince yourself. This was brought home to me at my next grass track meeting.

It was at Kirkby Stephen, which at that time was in the delightful county of Westmorland. The track was just out of town in lush meadows and it was expected that John Wallace, from Consett, would make it his meeting. Gentleman John never looked to be going fast and one look at his machine was enough to give an impression that he would be an also ran. But out on the track John was quick without being spectacular. The track suited my style so much that heat wins became final wins.

Back in the pits a hand on my shoulder followed by a soft voice in that lovely Weardale accent, said, "It's your meeting tonight Ken." It was John Wallace. It was almost like him saying, 'you've done it tonight, why don't you do it more often?'

I was now one of the'in-crowd' and I was taking home £11 10s. (£11.50p).

There were more meetings and better results and I was seeing more of an old school pal. He had put together a machine for grass track using a Rudge frame and engine but had now bought a speedway machine from a redundant rider with a view to progressing to Speedway himself. I suggested he joined me on my next trip to Belle Vue. He too worked in the motor trade not very far from me, so by loading the machines on a Sunday, we could make a rapid getaway after work,

It was to become a regular Monday trip and my skills at changing a 500cc JAP Speedway engine were being honed to perfection. By the time the training school was closing for the winter both Keith and I seemed to have amassed enough 'brownie' points to return next year.

At the end of the season, which had extended into October, I looked back with a certain amount of satisfaction. Machine reliability had improved and I could at last feel that the project seemed worthwhile. But I did miss the M20 with the sidecar. It had provided many miles of enjoyment and those that have experienced it, will agree that riding a motorcycle with a sidecar attached around a right hand bend can provide a great deal of pleasure.

At weekends the 250cc BSA was available, either to ride as solo, or alternatively, with Dad. Whenever he was riding pillion I still felt like the apprentice. There had been a scare during the summer due to the Suez crisis. It was threatened there would have to be petrol rationing and coupons were issued at the beginning of the year. But it was not rigorously applied in many parts of Britain and ended in May.

I was still writing letters to speedway promoters requesting a trial, but the replies did not equal the enquiries. I had noted in one magazine that speedway on the continent, while not booming, was active in Holland, Germany and France. It seemed the man behind the venture, acting as an agent for promoters, was former rider, Phil Bishop. By former I could perhaps mean founder, as Phil had been at the first speedway meeting held in Britain in February, 1928. Furthermore, he was still donning his leathers from time to time to make up team numbers. He had acquired the sobriquet, the 'King of Crash' due to the number of bones he had broken, but kept coming back to ride.

With an attitude nothing ventured, nothing gained, I wrote to Phil with a brief summary of my career, remembering to stress my contact with the Langton Brothers, against whom he had raced in the thirties. His reply, while not discouraging, did say that it could only be considered as a possible progression into speedway and that there was no easy money to be earned. As a final footnote, he added that for the new season, he would be making a trip to the Belle Vue Training School and would be in contact in due course.

For the 1958 season, The Speedway Control Board had no option but to form a single league for the remaining teams. The introduction of nationwide television had forced many tracks to close due to dwindling attendances. The first grass track meeting of the year took place at Esholt, near Bradford. This time, however, without any publicity from the local press. Someone started a rumour that Ken Mellor and Keith Morrison had been riding at Belle Vue Speedway and should not be allowed to compete. However, Clerk of the Course, John Whitaker, a vintage motorcyclist and speedway follower was of the opinion that our attendance at Belle Vue could hardly be considered professional and overruled the objection.

Our first visit to the Monday Training School needed some help from a 'sick grandmother' as we had to ask for half a day off work. Phil Bishop was hoping to be there so it was a chance not to be missed.

He told us he was representing a French promoter who was looking for two English riders to form the basis of his team for the new season, which began in May and ran until November. It started in the Regions of Brittany and Normandy, then through the summer months moving south until at the end of the season, the meetings were based around Perpignan and Marseilles.

Phil asked if we would be interested in signing up. Without knowing anything about the promotion of speedway in France, we said yes! In this life you sometimes have to give opportunity a helping hand to knock on your door!

There was of course shock and stunned silence when I arrived home and announced that I had signed up to go to France for six months to ride speedway. The silence was only broken when Mum asked, when? It would be in May and tickets and travel instructions would be forwarded. Until then there was much to prepare. The machine of course, what would be needed in terms of spares and luggage and resigning from my job.

The tickets would be from Folkestone to Boulogne, so we had to transport ourselves, plus two speedway machines from Leeds to the departure port. It began on a Monday morning at Leeds Central Station. These were still the days when you could wheel a motorcycle into the guards van, then remove it at King's Cross Station.

That was the easy part. The Boat Train left from Victoria Station across London in fashionable Belgravia. But we were in luck. A London cabbie and a Wimbledon Speedway fan saw the machines and asked where we were heading. He suggested he could take us one at a time as he saw no reason why a speedway machine would not go into his cab, cheerfully adding that he had once taken a donkey across London.

Keith went first leaving me on the station concourse, not knowing how long it would take. Twice I was approached by tourists wanting to have their photograph taken with me. As a silly aside, I have sometimes wondered if I still feature in some family album on a shelf in Kansas or Kentucky! Eventually, we were both standing on Victoria Station with machines and luggage safely on board.

Being a Boat Train and connecting with the sailings, there was only a short distance to the ship. The frightening part was the method of loading used, which consisted of a chain around the handlebars, then hoisted fifty feet before coming down into the hold. Drive on drive off ferries were still a daydream.

So far everything had worked smoothly. Then we arrived in Boulogne. Problem number one, so far as we could understand, there was no carrying space on the Paris train for our machines and they would have to follow separately. To wave goodbye to something that you have invested most of your savings in was not easy to do, nor was it helped by our lack of understanding of the language.

There was still a journey of over 400 miles to complete which involved a train to Paris, change stations, then a train to the Brittany Peninsular and the little town of Uzel. Which of course was not marked on our complimentary tourist map of France.

In Paris there was the Metro system to take us from Gare Du Nord to Gare Montparnasse. Having to figure out the route while coping with luggage, toolboxes and riding equipment, did not make us too popular and you did not need to know any French to understand the thoughts of the other passengers.

We were now travelling through the night with one more change of trains, which we had to ensure we stayed awake for, finally arriving at the small station of Uzel, which seemed a long way out of town. We were the only passengers alighting and there appeared to be no staff on duty. Then a door opened and someone appeared, who would now have to be described as 'vertically challenged'. He spoke and I answered with, "Anglais, no parle." He went back inside and brought an elderly lady. She spoke the word 'coffee' and made a drinking gesture. Now we were getting somewhere. Keith added, "There's nothing to this language lark."

We followed them inside and were beckoned to sit. Two large bowls of black coffee were placed in front of us. No milk or sugar but it tasted wonderful. Then I saw the wall poster stating Uzel Speedway. Sur piste cendree. I pointed to the poster then to ourselves, followed by a gesture of me riding a motorcycle. She gave an outcry of realisation and went into a rapid confab with the small gentleman, then went to the telephone. Keith was right. There was nothing to this language lark!

After a few moments she made the gesture of driving and held up ten fingers. We had finally arrived at Uzel and were already fluent in French gestures! We knew little about the promoter only his name was Victor Boston of Russian extraction, but spoke fluent French and less fluent English through a thick east European accent.

Phil Bishop had told us not to expect French speedway to be organised to the standards we knew in Britain. There was no league racing with individual teams. One promoter controlled everything, which included the race results. Everything was planned just to entertain the crowd with the riders all being paid the same money.

If there was a stadium in the town, this would be used, or a track would be built by the town council. All the receipts were divided three ways. A third to the town mayor or council leader, a third to the promoter and the remainder to be shared between the riders. In simple terms, the larger the crowd, the more we were paid.

It was nearer to thirty minutes before we heard a vehicle, then the door opened and in walked a tall slim blond haired fellow in his early twenties. "I am Claude." he said, holding out his hand. We made the introductions. Then I asked if he would thank the couple for their help. Whatever passed between them made him laugh and I enquired what had been said. "She says you are both very handsome." he replied.

He spoke good English but without the definite and indefinite articles, but he was understandable and he never stopped talking from leaving the station to arriving at the hotel. After checking in Claude took us to see the track which wasn't quite what we expected. The Town Hall square with a surface of ash and sand was being converted into an oval track.

The inside was marked with kerb stones but as yet there was no sign of a safety fence. Then Claude announced, "Boston wants to see you, he is in his office."

I said, "Why so informal? We thought he was Mr Boston."

"He's my Father I call him Boston!" he replied.

It was to be the first of many surprises, including his office in the town. This turned out to be the Café de Ville and there was one in most towns in France. If there wasn't, it would be the Café des Amis. It was an amazing sight to see the table littered with papers, bread, butter, fruit and biscuits. Everyday for at least two hours and all for the price of one cup of coffee, he held court, met clients and business associates, wrote letters and in our case, interview riders. It seemed that in France, once you left the urban centres, the town's cafe was the centre of the universe.

Victor Boston was not the image of a promoter we had imagined. His face was world weary and he moved awkwardly, the result of a broken leg in earlier years which had not been set by a doctor. We gathered he had left Russia at the time of the Revolution and spent many years in India and the Far East presenting his troupe of 'daredevil' acts from high wire to motorcycle stunts, being billed as, 'Les Bostons.'

His speedway operation now centred on his team of French and Spanish riders, augmented by two permanent English riders and a team of riders from England that would travel out to attend the bigger prestige meetings about every four weeks. Most of the local riders were also gathered in the cafe, so we had a chance to compare notes and size up the opposition.

The immediate concern was for our machines which we had last seen at Boulogne, however, no matter how lax life appeared to be, French Railways delivered them to the same station we had first arrived at and none the worse for the journey. They were given a thorough inspection by the local riders, wanting to know of any tuning hints or tips that we could pass on. We were also given a guarded warning by Claude to ensure our toolboxes were always padlocked as items such as spare piston rings, valves and spark plugs did have a habit of disappearing!

Mr Boston asked what we thought about the track, the length being around 250 yards and certainly the smallest both of us had ridden on, including grass tracks. No practice laps were allowed as this would give the public a free show and as every franc counted towards our earnings, we had to accept this. It was a case of the smallest engine sprocket in the spares box. However, as a means of publicising the Sunday meeting, we were going to be allowed to ride our machines through the streets on Saturday afternoon. One of many advantages of having the Town Mayor on your side!

But before that happened a meeting was called to run through the sequence of events on the day. It would start with all the riders being introduced to the crowd. There would then follow a simple formula of ten heats on the usual points scoring basis of 3; 2; 1; with the four highest scorers going forward to a final. Then came the lap record attempts with each rider trying to establish the fastest lap and if there was still time and the crowd were wanting more, there would be a 'Grand Challenge encounter' for the four highest points scorers.

Our first impression that we were in 'show business' came when Mr Boston said he wanted us to stay at the rear in each race, while making every effort to show that we were trying our best to overtake. It wasn't about winning, it was about entertainment. However, he informed us that we would be able to send match results each month to the overseas Editor at the Speedway Star offices in London. It was to prove one way of keeping our names in the public eye.

Because Keith and I had machines with much more visible chrome, we were chosen to lead the parade around the town following the publicity vehicle with loudspeakers blaring. All with the approval of the Gendarmes, despite having open exhausts and no brakes. Both of us were smiling at the thought of how far we would get if we tried it in Leeds City Centre! Nevertheless, crowds gathered and waved and even if they hadn't seen a speedway machine before, it seems the commentator built up our stature to an extent that I was billed as a European Champion, while Keith had just returned from a successful tour of Scandinavia.

On Sunday we were up and about early. First we had to modify the mixture control to cope with the lower quality alcohol fuel and found the easiest way was to stuff a duster in the air intake to act as a choke. It seems there was already some resentment among the other riders, believing that we would race ahead and make them appear inferior in front of their home crowd. The French riders were more concerned than the Spaniards who just shrugged it off with an attitude of 'all for one and one for all', but we decided to keep a close eye on one or two who did not seem convinced with our assurance that we would stay in the background.

Keith and I had discussed the situation and were of the opinion that if we were all being paid the same, why take any risks. Especially when we saw the concrete posts and iron rails that had been constructed to act as a safety fence. So this was our initiation to French speedway. Putting on an act was the easy part, all we had to do was pass and repass each other, then close up on the two riders in front with plenty of body swerving to indicate we were trying 101% to overtake them, especially on the last lap just before the chequered flag.

After three meetings of acting the part we began to feel like repertory actors who were stuck with the same play week after week, which was not helped by the other riders forming a 'them and us' situation. So it was with some relief that we looked forward to the next meeting in Normandy, when a team of riders from England would be joining us. This would make up a normal programme of sixteen riders over fourteen heats.

The meeting was to to be held in Alencon at the recently completed sports stadium. The town had witnessed fierce fighting during the Normandy conflict and many buildings still bore the scars. For the English team it was an easy drive from the port of Dieppe and two vehicles were used for machines and riders one of whom was Phil Bishop. Also along was another veteran, George Bason, who had also ridden pre war and was now just keeping his hand in with occasional second half rides and trips to the continent.

We mentioned to Phil about the home riders wanting to take the glory while we wallowed along behind and while he had every sympathy for us, he just summed it up with,

"Well we are all on the same money, so just be gentle with them." But he added, "Mind you if the mood takes me, I might make them work hard for it." Then with a grin he went back to preparing his machine.

With hindsight it was a moment I regret not prolonging and spending more time with him, for when the meeting was over and everyone was packing and loading equipment, I missed their actual departure from the stadium. I say regretted because that was last time I saw him. Twelve years later, Phil was one of five riders killed in what has become known as the 'Lokeren Disaster.' This was in Belgium and the team were heading back to the ferry, when their mini bus was in collision with a petrol tanker and two lorries. The driver of the mini bus also died. Phil was 58.

Another rider taking part in the meeting at Alencon was Eric Jolly and it was only while preparing the book manuscript, 57 years later, that I discovered he was a nephew of Eric Langton. Eric would be back again in two months. These contacts with riders from England were our main source of information about the speedway scene back home and as the year progressed, there were increasing rumours about a revival in the sport with a lower division being formed similar to the old Third Division.

For Keith and I this gave new hope that there may be opportunities with tracks reopening and teams looking for riders. We made sure our monthly missives to the Speedway Star were gently 'distorted' to ensure our names were mentioned in the copy. There were two more meetings in Normandy, at Mortagne, and La Ferte-Mace. Neither of which attracted large crowds, so the Francs were not exactly flowing freely.

We were now moving towards the Loire Valley and I have already made mention of Mr Boston's quirk for changing a rider's name and nationality if he thought it would stand out on any publicity material. He always employed someone to 'bill the town' a few days before our arrival and for this meeting just outside Le Mans, I became Tom Mellor from Washington, while Keith took on the role of, Herb Morrison from Scotland.

We both took the attitude of 'what's in a name' and if it brought paying customers, who were we to complain. What no one knew was that a few miles out of town was a French Military airbase and a NATO exercise was taking place involving two squadrons of American fighter aircraft. In addition to the air crews, they had also brought a compliment of ground crews and medical nurses.

The power of advertising had brought to the attention of the American Welfare Officer, that one of their countrymen was riding at the speedway meeting and he contacted the Promoter to say they would be bringing two buses of supporters, which would include a team of 'cheer leaders.' At this stage you may well be thinking of that timeless remark about something hitting the fan! It was more like a knock out blow with me on the receiving end.

I put it to Mr Boston that there was no way I could appear as an American citizen and there could be trouble. Unfortunately, he didn't see it that way. To him two buses with supporters could add up to five hundred Francs in gate receipts. I tried to explain that my accent would not convince anyone that I came from Washington, but he was insistent that nobody would mind and I could say my parents brought me to England at an early age.

It was my second protest in two days. Mr Boston's wife was German and had very little command of English. Her pronunciation of my name always came out in the form of 'Muller', with the obvious suggestion of German origin. It was certainly not the impression you wanted to convey in an area where less than fifteen years earlier, that nation had ruled with a very firm hand. It was even worse when she bellowed it from some distance away, making heads turn to see who was the respondent!

When Sunday arrived we went through the usual preparations. The track had been built inside a velodrome, or cycle track and the surface was a mixture of pea sized gravel and sand. The cycle track was banked so if you were to run off at the bends, there was a steep banking to check your progress. What I was dreading happened about an hour before the start. Two buses arrived full of military personal mostly in uniform, including the nurses along with six girls dressed in frills and skimpy skirts and twirling batons. These were my cheerleaders and were soon letting me and everyone else know about it.

Whatever opinion you have about Americans, they are adept at taking things in their stride and joining in with everything and everyone. The men wanted to know all about the speedway machines, while the girls mixed freely with no reticence amongst the riders, even asking the Spanish riders if it was more dangerous than bull fighting. I don't recall anyone asking about Washington and the girls in their frills chanted my name (Tom was my Dad's name actually) and kicked their legs in the air. There was to be just one problem. As the racing started and each time I went out for my heat, I was receiving more attention from one particular girl than seemed natural.

She was always there in the background. Asking about the race, the machine, what were my thoughts as I raced around. Overbearing was the only word to describe it and it was to continue after the meeting. Asking about my parents, was I religious, what did I think about war. It was with a great sigh of relief when I saw her board the bus and it disappear down the road.

Next morning, that same relief turned into near terror, for she was at the hotel waiting for me to arrive for breakfast. I had noted she had a quaint form of speaking, often using such words as, thou and thee. During the conversation she informed me she was a Quaker and did I know about them. I then had to sit through a brief history of the movement and how it had moved from England to America. She also explained why she was a military nurse, even though the Quaker movement were pacifists. All I could do was nod in agreement. I didn't have a clue what she was talking about.

She was still around after lunch when we were packing all the equipment and loading the lorry wanting to know which town we were going to and that she would like to visit. Also amidst all her rambling, she had asked me did I believe in wedlock. The situation was now dire. In modern parlance I suppose I was being 'stalked' but in 1958 I'm not sure what the word would have been. Even Mr Boston was becoming concerned. The last thing he wanted was the might of any military enquiry into his operation and personnel, not to mention his business finances.

She had been asking which town we were travelling to next and it was decided to make up a poster depicting a venue some thirty miles away in the opposite direction. I passed this to her and made some excuse about having to collect some spares from the railway station. In reality, I was being taken by Alberto, one of the Spanish riders, to the next town where I would check in and keep a low profile.

For the next meeting I was back to being just plain old Ken Mellor. We were still in the Loire Valley, near to the Town of Blois with it's historic chateau. Six English riders were booked, with veteran George Bason skippering the group. Also along on their first visits were Geoff Harris and Stan Tebby. Keith was becoming a little disillusioned with bringing up the rear each time. Or as he phrased it, "Always being the bridesmaid and never the bride."

He just happened to be featured in the first heat and beat everyone off the start line, only to splutter to a halt on the second lap. He had forgotten to turn the fuel on. He made up for his blunder in the record lap attempts by setting the fastest time and winning himself a bottle of Champagne. I had been pestering a number of riders for information about the new tracks planned to open in 1959 and was now beginning to compile a dossier of contact names and details. I would only have one more opportunity as there was a final meeting before we moved too far south and out of economical range of the Channel Ports.

This was at Nogaro, a town about sixty miles north of Lourdes. On the first day as we arrived, I thought I could see a bank of cloud on the horizon, but it turned out to be our first glimpse of the Pyrenees. The Town Council were very much behind this meeting from building the track to picking up the hotel bill for the visiting riders. Once again they were led by George Bason, with whom I had now developed a friendly rapport, not knowing that within a few months I would be living almost next door to him. Of the other riders, Ernie Baker, Geoff Harris, Arthur Hewitt and Ted Spittles would become riding colleagues in the 1959 season.

When they first arrived there was some concern over the track size. They had been informed that it would be 420 metres, giving the impression of a large track. The organiser had given them the outer perimeter measurement, whereas in reality, the inner white line distance was 260 metres. Fortunately, most of them had a selection of sprockets which enabled a suitable ratio to cope with the small track.

The surface was a mixture of ash and sand into which had been mixed quantities of cement and sawdust. The whole track was then watered and rolled giving quite a firm base.

After the first few heats it became clear that the English riders were enjoying themselves and not complying with the usual arrangement of playing second fiddle. One of the French riders, best described as an egotist, was incensed at being soundly beaten into forth place and promptly returned to the starting line, took out the Union Jack from the array of International flags and broke the pole across his knee, then hurled it towards the pits. All to cheers from his supporters.

Keith and I didn't want to be left out of the rout so in the last race before the lap record attempts, Keith made a good start and played 'cat and mouse' with two Spanish riders, while I played catch up at the rear until the last bend, then dived between them and crossed the line as near a dead heat with Keith as I could make it.

Life had now become somewhat sedentary. After each Sunday meeting we followed the same routine of loading the machines, packing the suitcase, a late meal which would often last two hours and an early night. We had begun making bets as to what the next 'office' would be called. Café de Ville, Café du Sport, Café du Pont or Café des Amis. Adding in a day for machine maintenance still left a lot of time to fill.

Back in the fifties there was a popular song entitled, 'Life gets Tedious,' echoing everyday events that don't change a thing. It may appear to have been an idyllic lifestyle but it was not yet achieving that ambition I started out with. With all the information I had amassed from the English riders, the plan was now to begin contacting the new tracks listed to open for the new season, ensuring I mentioned the coverage we had been getting in the European pages of the speedway press.

I recollect sending over a dozen letters using my home address as the season in France only had around six weeks left. We were moving south again, this time to Tarbes which was only thirty miles from the Spanish border and in the foothills of the Pyrenees. The Spanish riders were certainly more cheerful, even inviting us to visit their homes.

It had always been the policy to use minor roads as we journeyed from town to town. The reason was due to a heavy police presence on all major roads due to Algerian terrorists causing trouble over disputed Home Rule demonstrations. One look at the elderly Peugeot lorry with a tarpaulin covered load, would be enough to spur the Police de la Route into action. We were never sure if we and the Spanish riders were classed as tourists or migrant workers and the last thing Mr Boston wanted was a large scale investigation into his business affairs.

So when we travelled in the cab, it was on the understanding that if we should be stopped, we would not speak unless spoken to and if we had to show our Passports, we were just holidaymakers. It was all very 'cloak and dagger.'

The track at Tarbes was again within a Velodrome with a banked cycle track forming the run off area. In fact it was so steep that when putting in a few practice laps, we were able to ride close to the top and yet be almost horizontal. To feel the G-Force on your whole body and machine as it was being pressed against the track made me admire those Brooklands riders of the twenties who touched three figures on vintage machinery.

During the actual racing we of course stayed within the confines of the ash surface and as we had now resorted to our roles of 'bringing up the rear,' leaving the Spanish and French riders to bask in their victories, we were back in everyones good books. This included an English family who were on a caravan holiday and insisted that we join them in the evening for a meal to compensate for our good efforts and 'better luck next time,'

As it was the best meal we had tasted in five months, we didn't have the heart to enlighten them.

The countryside in the foothills of the Pyrenees was magnificent. Small lanes just disappearing out of sight, over which we were assured many escaping British prisoners of war had been led to safety. It was the sort of claim we had become used to over the last few months. We never ceased to be amazed how many people, on hearing we were English, had belonged to the resistance movement.

Alberto Sirvan was one of the Spanish riders with a passable knowledge of English. He also had a Gnome-Rhone with a sidecar which he towed behind his caravan. It was built very much in the style of a BMW with a pressed steel frame, having a capacity of 750cc. It had tremendous hill climbing ability too, when four of us set off just to see how high we could go up the Pyrenees.

We climbed past an altitude marker post showing 1000m but the route was now becoming less defined. Above us in the distance could be seen an outpost with the French Tricolore showing, which Alberto confirmed was a Customs Post. So we were not going to be able to escape to Spain over this route! The return journey downhill was not without some hair-raising moments too.

Alberto promised us a trip into Spain to see his brother-in-law who was one of the top rank bullfighters, but first we had to make our way towards Perpignan for the next meeting and our first sighting of the Mediterranean Sea.

It was not an easy journey. There was only one road by way of Toulouse and Narbonne and it was bound to be heavily patrolled by the police. But this was the least of our problems. On the way the rear axle began to make a grinding noise, which Keith diagnosed as the teeth on the crown wheel stripping. He suggested stopping before more damage was done, but Mr Boston had other plans.

It was sounding more expensive as each mile went by. Claude had been telling us that Perpignan was a, "Big town, plenty people, much money."

Keith added, "It may need much money to fix the rear axle."

But Mr Boston was resourceful. He had been on the phone to the next town of Carcassonne and found a garage that not only had the same model lorry, but were prepared to sell the rear axle. All we had to do now was hope and pray it would keep turning for a few more miles.

It was a roomy cab and as we drove along Keith and I were reminded of something akin to a Laurel and Hardy comedy. Mr Boston was sitting in the driving seat with his hands on the wheel and could barely see past the radiator. Claude, who had no driving licence, was sitting to his right with his feet controlling accelerator, brake and clutch, plus changing gear and his right hand on the lower rim of the steering wheel. To the outside observer, Mr Boston appeared to be in complete control.

So the last thing we wanted to see were two police motorcyclists by the roadside. In less than a mile we were overtaken and given the signal to pull to the side of the road. We put on our best smiles as they came alongside. But their concern was for the smoke that was coming from the rear axle.

Claude was already outside in case he had to translate anything to us. But we heard the name, Henri Bovard, the garage we were heading for. Then there was the sound of laughter, always a good indicator that you are not in trouble. Then with nothing more than a wave and wishing us, "Bonne Chance," they were on their way.

Claude translated that they knew the garage owner and hoped the axle would last a few more miles. Had they known, they could have filled two note books with offences and probably received a commendation from their Chief!

We were within a mile of the garage and climbing a hill when the engine suddenly began racing and all drive was lost. So near and yet so far. Engaging first gear with the handbrake on was barely holding the load, hence the wedge shape block under the drivers seat for such an occasion. Alberto, who had been following at a discreet distance had now caught up and suggested using his Citroen as a tow for the short distance to the top.

With everything ready he tried to take the strain, but it was just too much for the car. Then he suggested the Gnome-Rhone outfit pulling at the front if one of us could drive the Citroen. I was game to try and on a shout from Alberto, I let the clutch in as he started forward. We were moving and we kept moving to the top of the hill and straight onto the garage forecourt.

Henri Bovard spoke some English and told us he had twice been to the Earls Court Motor Show. His mechanics had the spare axle ready but it was going to be down to Keith and I to fit it. The first problem was unloading the lorry as our jacks would not lift the weight. Once again it was Henri to the rescue with an offer of under cover storage for the machines, plus arranging for overnight accommodation in the village.

There was some reasonable daylight left, so a start was made removing all the brake pipes and fittings, along with the drive shaft joint. Most of the bolts were in reasonable order with nuts that would turn easily, so we undid all those that were easily accessible and clocked off. Tomorrow was another day and a meal and a good nights sleep would prepare us for the hard part.

We made an early start hoping to have the old axle out before the sun rose too high. It was going to be down to Keith and I to get the job done, as we were unlikely to have any help from the other riders, who were noticeable by their absence. Two bottle jacks lifted the chassis and the axle was dragged clear leaving some preparatory cleaning to ensure a smooth changeover.

I was under the body removing the usual road dirt when I heard a cracking sound and saw to my horror that the concrete under one of the jacks was crumbling. I dived to one side and a few seconds later the lorry slipped off the other jack. When I look back on that incident after almost sixty years, it makes me realise that life is a very fine line that separates the difference between an accident and a near miss.

To be fair, Alberto and two other Spanish riders did offer their help and by 6pm the lorry was back on the road. As a way of showing his appreciation, Mr Boston took us into Carcassonne for a meal at a restaurant which was a cut above the usual Café de Ville.

Next day we trundled into Perpignan around midday. It was as we had been told, a large town with a population of over one hundred thousand. Keith and I did our, by now, weekly tally based on the theory that, if half a percent of the people turn out on Sunday, we should be in the money! It rarely worked out that way. Perpignan was a sprawling town that seemed to have missed most of the tourists heading towards the border and the Spanish resort of Barcelona. Being ten miles from the Mediterranean didn't help either.

By now we had become almost fluent in some phrases. A popular one that was needed as we drove into each new town and looking for the stadium was, "Excusez-moi, La stade de ville?" Claude took in the directions, while one of us added a convincing, "Merci." But it was to be our downfall a week later.

First impressions of the stadium were good. It was surrounded by strong fencing which reduced the risk of 'freebies' and there were two reasonable sized grandstands. Around the outside of the rugby pitch was a disused athletics track, which although now used for training purposes, showed little evidence of the original cinder surface.

We had arrived at a bad time. In fact we became embroiled in an argument between the organising council and the Club Committee over the lifting of turf that had been laid at the corners of the pitch and extended onto the track. The Club were of the opinion that it could be left in place and ridden over. But the French riders, in a very demonstrative manner, made it clear that this was speedway racing and not moto cross, even going so far as suggesting that the two riders from 'Angleterre' should have the final decision.

All of a sudden we were all one team and our opinion meant something. There was little point in disagreeing and it would be to our advantage, so we emphatically said, "It has to go!" The Club would not accept that and were not prepared to allow their ground staff to be used, neither would they allow outsiders to remove any turf. The situation was reaching deadlock.

By Saturday there had been no progress in the negotiations and it looked as if the riders had lost the argument. The turf was still in position and would have to be ridden over, there was certainly no way around it at racing speeds.

By Sunday morning, Keith and I were in no mood for heroics and we took our time over breakfast. Both machines were ready and as the meeting started at 3pm; we sauntered off towards the town centre. When we arrived back at the stadium, Claude confronted us and asked, "Was it you two?" I asked him what was he talking about and he then went into an excited description about the turf being removed during the night.

Sure enough, the two affected corners were now clear and ready for racing, we were also able to provide a reasonable alibi proving that we had not left our hotel after dinner. So far no one from the rugby club had appeared and there was now only an hour before racing began. Mr Boston was showing some agitation as he fully expected repercussion from the rugby committee and if he did have to pay any damages it would presumably, effect the share paid to the riders.

The meeting started on time and with Keith and I providing the usual excitement from behind, we soon had the crowd showing their allegiance to the French and Spanish riders. There were even some jeers when Keith was awarded the Cup for the fastest lap time. It was of course the same cup that had started the season in Brittany!

Most of the crowd had gone and we were loading the machines on the lorry when Alberto Sirvan rushed up and said, "Get in my car, I have to get you both out of town."

It seemed that members of the rugby club had arrived to check if the meeting had gone to plan, seen the turf lifted from the corners and immediately assumed it was the work of the 'English' riders and were out for vengeance.

We did not need a second invitation and both jumped into the rear of his Citroën and kept out of sight while he nonchalantly drove out of the stadium. Once clear he explained he was taking us to his Brother-in-law who had a hacienda in the foothills of the Pyrenees. He had of course promised to take us to see him earlier, but we didn't expect the reason for this trip to be fugitives from a team of rugby bruisers.

We were now heading inland towards the mountains and the border town of Puigcerda, which was only twenty miles from Andorra. Alberto had already telephoned our time of arrival and although Luco was away at a bullfight, we would be made welcome by his wife, Pilla. Our first glimpse of the ranch was stunning, looking like something from a Hollywood 'western'. From the entrance gate to the house was at least a mile, then in every direction were magnificent views of the mountains. Pilla, who spoke impeccable English, wanted to know more about us and our racing adventures and of course neither Alberto or ourselves mentioned the rugby stadium incident that was the reason for the visit.

All the time we were making small talk, we were surrounded by ponies nudging and nuzzling to see if we had any treats about us. Pilla asked if we rode and laughed when we assured her yes, but only motorcycles. We were shown inside where a light meal had been prepared and were shocked to find the table almost drooping under the weight of food. If there was an equivalent Spanish word for clambake it didn't show up in my tourist phrase guide.

It was a warm September evening as we sat on the veranda and marvelled at the view. It could easily have been the setting for James Hilton's book, Lost Horizon and the imaginary place in the mountains known as Shangri-La. Our musing was interrupted by a group of gauchos returning from their days work. Sitting on the boss's veranda must have made us important, for each one called a greeting or gave a polite gesture as they passed. Keith, with his dry humour, added, "I wonder if we are sleeping in their 'bunkhouse'"

One of the house staff showed us to the guest lodge via a covered walkway where our room was being made ready. It was equal if not better to any hotel we had stayed at over the last four months and by comparison it made the 'café de Villes' of France look like, a bunkhouse! Tomorrow we were off to see the fighting bulls and would be meeting Luco, who was expected home in the early hours, hopefully in a fit state after the bullfight.

Around 8am there was a knock on the door and coffee and toast arrived by courtesy of Alberto. He said Luco had arrived home safely and was looking forward to meeting us any time after 10am. As he was leaving he asked, "Do you want to ride to the farm or be driven." My answer was, "What do you think?" He just shrugged his shoulders.

Luco made an impression the moment he entered the room. He was tall, slim, bronzed by the sun and his English was perfect, with just a hint of an accent on certain words. He opened the conversation with, "Before you ask, I came to no harm yesterday." Then continued by asking how we faced danger and had we received any serious injuries. When it came to putting someone at their ease, he must have written the guide book.

We were driven in style to the stud farm in his individually built Facel-Vega which was the last of the French builders of luxury cars. Alberto sat in front next to the driver, while Keith and I sank into opulence at the rear with Luco, who was asking about our racing careers and life in England. The one thing he never asked us about during our stay, was what our opinions were on bull fighting. In view of the way we were treated while in his company, I may have found it difficult to give a truthful answer.

The black fighting bull is bred for aggression and ultimate death. Even with my face no more than three feet away and solid steel bars between us, one of them was intent on attacking me. It's whole body reaction and eyes suggested an inbred hatred for the human form. I think I hurt Luco's pride when I asked if he secreted a pistol in his tunic in case the cape and sword should ever prove insufficient.

What I did admire about him was how he treated his workers from Ranch Foreman to those doing the most menial of tasks. It was a very informal relationship despite his fame and wealth. Before leaving we saw the young apprentice bullfighters practicing their moves on selected young bulls. This was a twofold exercise for it not only honed their skills, but allowed the head breeder to assess the bull's reaction when it's time came to enter the ring.

On the way back to the vehicle, Luco stopped to talk to a young man who was very badly deformed. As he spoke we saw him pass some money over and place a hand briefly on his shoulder. He told us that his injuries had been received during his first public appearance when only twenty two. He had been tossed by the bull and severely gored.

Over a leisurely lunch, all Luco wanted to hear was about speedway racing and how we approached the 'moment of truth'. He went on to explain it was the moment we lean the machine in to a bend at speed against an opponent.

For him, his moment of truth came as he went for the final kill with the bull still capable of one more charge. His words were, "Either I die or the bull dies." It was a most sobering thought. For the rest of the day he was occupied with business affairs, leaving Keith and I, along with Alberto to practice our skills at trials riding with some small but very lively machines made by Montesa, a name then unknown to me.

Alberto had been in touch with Mr Boston, who was now based some miles north of Perpignan, and we were to rejoin the group the next day as we began the last two months of the season by moving around the coast down as far as Avignon and Marseilles. When we came to bid our farewells to Luco and Pilla, I jokingly asked if there were any vacancies for ranch hands so pleasant had been our stay. He laughed and said, "I will add your names to the long list of candidates."

As we headed back to France after sampling the 'high life' we had to re-adjust to a diet more in keeping with the parlous existence we had been leading. We were making our way to Agde for the next meeting. In 1958 it looked a pitiful area of mud flats and marsh and the town was nothing to shout about. It had all the makings of a poorly attended meeting with the resultant low share out for the riders.

I recall meeting someone around the time of the Millennium who had a time share apartment there and he marvelled about the shopping malls, marinas and holiday homes. It just proves that old saying, 'you turn your back for forty years and they rebuild the place'!

For this meeting it was the usual arrangement with the town council. They would build the track, the surface of which could be anything from sand and gravel to the dredgings from the mud flats and the town mayor would pocket his share of the takings. If by chance anyone in his family should be in the food business, this ensured they had the exclusive catering franchise too. Nepotism is the same the world over.

In actual fact the track turned out to be very ridable and being no more than three hundred yards, provided some good races for the crowd. As predicted, they numbered less than five hundred which was probably due to the hot weather. The Mediteranean could be a strong business competitor when it came to attracting the public. To ease his frustration, Keith did his last lap, last bend trick to win the final race, which drew the usual contempt from the French riders back in the pits. Claude later translated as much as his English would allow and the gist was the English were a race of 'porridge drinkers.' We could only assume that something was lost in the translation!

We were now heading towards the Departement Bouches du Rhône where it seemed that Mr Boston was something of a hero figure, certainly in a small town near Avignon. This was where he had lived during the second war and with his command of the German language had been a pillar of the community in helping local people through difficult times. This was where he usually wintered at the end of the racing season, along with some of the French riders.

The next meeting was at Sete, just south of Montpellier, and was again close to the sea, so even with a population of thirty thousand, good weather could limit the crowd. Alberto had a friend in town with a repair workshop, so an offer of servicing facilities for the machines was too good to turn down. Even though the racing had not been too stressful over the months in France, there were all the usual checks and adjustments to be made.

Over the past few weeks I had been making some tentative enquiries by post to some of the track contacts I had been given and in amongst a pile of letters and magazines from Dad and Mum was one from the team manager of Aldershot Speedway. This was one of the revived tracks that were opening next season in the re-formed Southern Area League. At this stage it was only a suggested meeting when I arrived back in England, but it was pleasing to note that my name had been noted in the Continental column in one of the magazines.

Keith had been reluctant to write to promoters being of the opinion that the only way was to turn up at a track with your machine and leathers and show them what you could do. While I couldn't argue with his logic, I have always believed in doing some preparatory work first. Or as the old Chinese saying goes, 'He who wants to catchee birdie must throw down some seed first.'

Sete proved to be a successful meeting, being incorporated as part of the Town's annual celebrations. With a good firm surface already in place and a substantial safety fence erected, it had all the hallmarks of an English third division stadium. Perhaps the only thing missing was the greyhound track. Nevertheless, the racing provided what the crowd wanted and it was my turn to take the cup for the fastest lap time.

The route from Sete was going to be tiresome. The main roads were heavily policed due to the proximity of Marseilles and any vehicle could be stopped at random, just what our dual control drivers did not want. So it was back to secondary roads and country lanes as we made our way to Mr Boston's home town of Isle-sur-la-Sorgue, twelve miles due east of Avignon. We were booked to ride there in November, which would be part of the towns Armistice celebrations, but before that date there were two meetings further up the Rhone Valley.

We were not sure what to expect as we drove into 'la-Sorgue'. It was certainly not the inactive town we expected and it boasted a station on the main line from Marseilles to Paris which would be our departure point in November. On the edge of town we drew up outside a large house which, like so many others had seen better times and badly in need of renovation. An elderly lady was coming to the gate and already babbling greetings and utterances of joy, soon to be joined by others of varying ages.

Mr Boston and Claude became lost in the cluster of embraces and greetings and were joined by two of the French riders as everyone seemed to be talking at once. As Keith and I stood smiling, Claude indicated who we were and we received a chorus of "Bon Jours" as we followed everyone else into the huge kitchen. The table was covered with cake, bread, fruit and of course various bottles of wine along with a huge coffee pot. The down side was three cats had free access to the table and food surfaces.

It looked like being a long session, so we filled our plates and wandered into the garden, only to be joined by the cats who must have sensed we might be a soft touch for titbits. I have never been a cat lover, Keith was even less so and he had the perfect deterrent which must have been left over from his childhood years. Filling his mouth with coffee he was able to emit a thin jet of liquid perfectly on target. The flies were an even bigger nuisance!

Alberto came out to join us, he obviously felt out of things too, adding that they were already reliving the liberation of France and the fall of the Vichy Government that had controlled this area during the occupation. We had both taken a liking for Alberto. He was not brash nor pompous and he was an excellent mechanic. It was this that prompted our idea to pass on our engine spares to him before we left for England. Although he could hold his own with the other French and Spanish riders, to get the best possible performance out of a JAP speedway engine, they did need regular attention to, piston rings, valves and spark plug. Our plan was to make the presentation to him at the final meeting.

For the next four days we saw little of Claude or his father. It seems there was much catching up to be done with many friends. Claude held court in the evening as everyone listened spellbound to his stories of the past twelve months. It seems we were given a glowing reference and we always knew when we were being discussed by all the heads that turned to take in this pair of foreigners. We later found out that we had been portrayed as former world champions. On one occasion of head turning and scrutinisation, it seems someone had enquired if we were married and how many children did we have. What a life of make believe we were leading.

For the next race meeting, we were heading north to the town of Nyons. This was situated in the Alpes du Daupine and if the racing was not going to be spectacular, then the scenery certainly made up for it with stunning views of the Alps, most of them rising to over 10,000 feet. Being an area that many tourists headed for, Claude was predicting a big crowd. He had a habit of rubbing his finger and thumb together while saying, "Plenty money." By now we could have easily chorused back and said, "Yea,Yea, we've heard it all before." Only that good old-fashioned English trait of dignity stopped us. The past months had revealed to us that, although he was an amiable and good looking sort, mainstream education seemed to have passed him by and he was certainly lacking in advanced reading and numeracy.

Nyons was indeed a tourist centre and the council had arranged for a display stand in the market square on the Saturday before race day. Three or four of the French riders came along, while Keith had his bike on display and to drum up some business, he would start it and treat the crowd to the open exhaust while Claude did his spiel about the international field of riders that were appearing on Sunday. On this occasion I was allowed to keep my English identity!

The local paper did a feature piece on the event, even using a photograph showing English, French and Spanish riders and their machines. While we were standing around soaking up the 'pomp', a mother and daughter approached and said they were from Wakefield and that they sometimes attended speedway meetings at Odsal Stadium, Bradford. Once again it illustrated that theory of synchronism and the incalculable odds that bring about such meetings in our lives. Adding their journey to our odyssey and the chances of meeting in a market square of an obscure French town on a Saturday afternoon in 1958 is a question for greater minds than mine.

As we chatted, they told us that one of their foremost complaints about the country were the toilets, with which I had to agree. For me it had begun at Gare du Nord station in Paris where I was confronted by a lady attendant while wanting to spend a'Centime'. It appears the husband had gone off to look at some ancient ruins and their femininity for a bargain and shops had brought them to the square, along with a familiar sound of a speedway machine being warmed up. They were sold on the idea of attending the meeting and adding their support, so for once we were not going to be riding in front of a totally hostile crowd.

The stadium was small which meant the track was no more than 250 yards, but it would ensure close racing and make our task easy when it came to playing the part of eager opposition. We were still likening ourselves to a couple of old repertory actors travelling around just taking our cues and wandering on and off the stage. Keith suggested during the interval that we should both come through on the last lap of the last race just to please the English supporters. All three of them!

I went along with his idea, even if it did create more accusations of being 'porridge drinkers' from the French riders. Even after five months there had been no thawing in their attitude towards us. Which was not the case with the Spanish riders, who were only hampered by their lack of English, apart from Alberto. As we went out for the last race, the favourite, who we had nicknamed, 'Desboards,' the name of a big scrap yard we had seen back in Normandy, was already working the crowd with waves and gestures, so it was going to be a joy to prick his ego. On the third lap I slipped into second place and held off the other French rider, while Keith lined himself up for his usual last bend 'around the outside' trick. As he did, I opened the throttle and we came out of the bend side by side and crossed the line to a stunned silence from the crowd.

Our supporters numbered three, as the husband was also attending and his lovely Wakefield accent was such a comfort to us amongst the jeers and sneers. I had noticed Mr Boston was not looking too overjoyed as he spoke with a number of the town council members. We later found out that 'Desboards', having being predicted as the outright winner, was to present the prizes at a local function in the town hall and we had blighted his self-esteem. Alberto kept us informed with all the gossip that was being thrown our way, which again seemed to lose something in the re-telling but covered subjects such as, roast beef, Queen Victoria and Big Ben. They were not noted for a sense of humour.

As we travelled to the next town, our English humour was working overtime as we came up with more and more funny lines based on the name. The problem was, we were the only ones who could see the funny side, which just goes to show that humour does not travel too well. Nevertheless, we thought it was hilarious and became convulsed with laughter. The town had the unfortunate name of Die, which gave rise to such parodies as, "We are all going to Die." "Is this the way to Die.» «Can you tell me the best way to Die.» «Sorry I can't stop I'm going to Die.»

After fifty miles, our pair of dual drivers could stand no more and Claude with an obvious reaction of anger, switched on the radio. That was fine by me, but he suffered from an infuriating habit I have come across many times with people of little patience. He could not bear to listen to one station for more than thirty seconds and was constantly turning the retuning knob.

Die nestled in the foothills of the western Alps and did not look like the sort of venue that would bring people out in large numbers. The two people employed to 'bill the town' would need to work hard with posters in all the prominent places if this meeting was going to show a profit. It had also been a torturous journey along some very steep roads and there had been several delays to allow the radiator to cool down.

Keith and I were mindful of the mechanics who had checked the replacement rear axle several weeks ago before we had fitted it. They had given an assurance that the brake linings were in good order and it was always pleasing to note on the steep down hill sections, a good firm pedal was always present without the need for pumping. Whether the handbrake would have held was a different matter as we were way over the weight carrying limit, but we had a contingency plan in case of pending disaster. At the first hint of trouble, Keith was to throw open the door and leap clear, with me, hopefully, close behind.

We were taken to see the site selected for the track and to meet 'Mr Big.' It seems that he was putting up all the money to stage the meeting and probably taking the biggest cut too. His English was good and he preferred to take our advice as to the size and layout of the track, rather than Mr Boston's. He also put us in a most unenviable position when he took us to one side and asked if Claude or Mr Boston could be trusted and did we have a financial stake in the promotion.

At least we could be honest about the second part of his query. All we could do was advise him that we had joined the organisation in May and still had four meetings to complete by mid-November. That sounded honest enough to both of us. Even if he did think he was going to make a 'quick buck,' he certainly put his money where his mouth was and had the track completed within a day, the surface comprising coarse sand mixed with cement dust, watered then rolled.

'Mr Big' had not been seen since work on the track was finished and as he did not appear on the day of the meeting, there was naturally some unease about his financial commitment to fund the event. The basic material costs for the track, in addition to the hire of equipment and labour had amounted to a substantial sum and looking at the size of the crowd, it appeared as if there would be a deficit.

Everything was going smoothly regarding the running of the meeting and the crowd were certainly getting good value for their money. This included two accidents, which although they looked far more serious than the outcome, provided that element of excitement to the danger of competitive motor sport.

When the interval came I went round to the rear of the stand where George, the man who went around sticking advertising posters to prominent sites, had his caravan. He always had hot and cold drinks available and as I was helping myself, I could hear announcements over the public address along with jeers from the crowd. I hurried back to the pits to find a mass of Gendarmes and officials everywhere.

Keith gave me an urgent wave to join him where I found Mr Boston and Claude involved in an argument with someone over the ownership of all the racing machines, the excavator and roller, plus all the ancillary equipment. I finally found Alberto to ask what had happened and was told that 'Mr Big', otherwise known as Raymond le Bois, had been arrested for diamond smuggling and transferring illegal money. Or what would now be known as money laundering. The purpose of the police visit was to seize all the equipment, including our machines on the belief that everything had been funded by him.

The authorities also wanted the money that had been paid at the turnstile as part of the seizure, but found this had already disappeared. Not due to any quick thinking by Mr Le Bois, but by Mrs Boston, who had reacted to the initial police raid with a certain amount of alacrity and placed the bag of takings in her caravan.

Having to deal with foreign officials to try and convince them that we were the legitimate owners of our machines was not an easy task and once again a huge debt of thanks had to be conveyed to Alberto for his assistance. By good fortune we had retained our travel 'Carnet de Passage en Douanes' in our toolboxes, so were able to provide immediate proof of ownership, including the port of entry into France. However, the French and Spanish riders, even with no language barrier, still had difficulty before it was agreed to release their property.

We stayed in Die an extra night instead of returning to our base. Mr Boston had arranged to pay the local suppliers and workers, thus ensuring they were not out of pocket. A gesture which elevated him several places in our estimation. What happened to any local councillors who were expecting something in a plain brown envelope was unsure. Maybe Mr Boston suggested they became creditors of Raymond le Bois.

For the return journey to Isle sa la Sourge, we took the precaution to include extra containers of water and it was not long before we were topping up the radiator to keep pace with the steaming cap. For the remainder of the trip, we enjoyed the local newspapers coverage of their big crime story about Le Bois, even describing Keith and I as 'le cendree pilotes from Angleterre'. Claude kept repeating one word to describe him. Just how he knew he had been born out of wedlock I had no idea!

For the next few days we had little to do. We were now into late October and with only four meetings left, we were beginning to feel 'demob happy'.

Maybe the past months were taking their toll as we reflected on some of the events and escapades. It had certainly been a roller coaster ride. The Bostons' were still revelling in their wartime recollections, so with the help of Alberto we made several trips to Avignon to enjoy some of the culture, including a walk on the bridge that had become famous in the song, 'Sur le Pont d'Avignon', sung by Jean Sablon. Which just happened to be one of Dad's many 78rpm records I had grown up with.

Le Pontet was a small town on the approach to Avignon and we had already passed through several times. We had also visited the stadium which served as a bull ring. However, in this part of France the bull lived to fight another day. They had a more civilised sport known as 'Les Courses Camargaises' where the matador tried to place a ring over the horn of the charging bull. No mean feat when you have nothing to defend yourself with and dressed only in a gaudy silk costume.

On the day of the actual meeting and while on our way to the stadium, we were involved in an incident, or as the French would say, contretemps, which could have been far more serious than the actual outcome. Alberto had been having ignition trouble with his car and we found him stranded just out of town. One of the other French riders had attached a thin steel cable to the car and was about to set off towing him with around ten feet of tow line and suggested we followed as back up.

On the approach to Le Pontet we were slowed by heavy traffic due to a local cycle race and in no time were surrounded by cyclists trying to find a way through. Two of them thought they had found a short cut in front of Alberto's car and headed for the gap, never seeing the slender tow cable. Alberto saw them and made a rapid brake application just as they collided with the tow line, but the effect was to pull the rear bumper from the front vehicle.

Braking is all about thinking distance and Claude was slow to react from his co-driver position with the result we hit the rear of Alberto's car. This was followed by an impact of someone hitting the rear of the lorry. The 'police de la Route' were quickly on the scene and came to the conclusion that the two cyclists were the cause of the whole affair and were dismissing their protests that the towing vehicle should have displayed warning signs. Their only concern was getting the traffic moving and with only superficial damage to the lorry, we were able to continue to the stadium.

Being circular, the bull ring was not an ideal place for a conventional speedway track, but the surface was a near perfect texture and with nothing at stake, we adopted an attitude that, 'things could have been worse'. The meeting ran to the usual race format and as Alberto had stayed at the scene of the accident, one of the other Spanish riders filled in with extra rides. It was an enjoyable meeting with a sizeable crowd, making the riders share of the gate money the best for a number of weeks. Keith and I had now decided that, being so close to the end of the season, there was no point in taking any risks so we were happy to let the French and Spanish riders battle for honours amongst themselves.

Back at Isle sa la Sourge, Mr Boston's office was in the old house and he was now busy arranging possible the biggest meeting of the tour. This was to be at Marseilles and we had frequent reminders from Claude that the population was a million people, although by now we had become experienced enough to know that, by halving anything he said was nearer reality. The track was to be around another rugby pitch which sounded like the usual 'Persian market' with club officials on the make, along with the odd councillor or two. However, Mr Boston went to town with the publicity posters and even placed an advertisement in the local paper, so it had all the makings of a 'nice little earner'.

But it was not to be. On the Friday night before the meeting a dinner dance was held in the clubhouse and in the early hours the whole complex was destroyed by fire, reputed to have started in the kitchen area. This was a financial disaster for Mr Boston as there was no such thing as insurance to cover his operation. Keith and I were not too overjoyed either. We were hoping this meeting would provide a little boost to our earnings before departing for home and there were now only two meetings left, both in small sized towns.

We now had several days to fill and Claude proposed a bus ride to Marseilles, even suggesting we stay over as he could negotiate a cheap rate for accommodation. This made sense as anyone with a foreign accent could be ripped off in such a huge commercial centre. Where the bus stopped was probably the equivalent of Wapping or Mile End Road in London. It was certainly not the sort of area you would take your Mother to!

Claude stopped at the first cafe which looked conventional enough. Tables outside with coloured umbrellas, men were drinking coffee or wine and there was a steady flow of customers going in and out. What could be more pleasant, even more so when we were told the price of a room for the three of us. The lady who led the way had a nice matronly appearance along with a fixed smile which never changed, even when we handed over our Francs. Still the room was ample for our needs, even if the carpet was threadbare and the bed covers looked as if they had not seen the laundry for some considerable time. I had also noticed that the door frame had been forced open recently. But in an attempt to cancel out all the imperfections, on the bedside table was a blue plate with an orange.

Only a few doors from the cafe was a cinema showing Humphrey Bogart in 'The African Queen' and as Claude had not seen it he wanted to go in. He was under the impression that it would have been dubbed into French and he would need to try and explain the story, however, the tables were turned, for it was screened in English with sub-titles along the bottom. So Keith and I enjoyed a first class film show, while the rest had to squint and peer at the bottom of the screen. This was followed by a magnificent fish meal at one of the dozens of quayside cafes.

It was around ten o'clock when we returned to the cafe to find, as Americans would say, 'the joint was jumping'. There now seemed to be more women than men which should perhaps, have given us some indication of the real purpose of the establishment, but what did two raw lads from Leeds know about cafe life in Marseilles. When we were first in the room, I don't suppose any of us noticed the other door and where it might have led. Our suspicions were first aroused as we going up the stairs. Coming out of our room was a girl and two men, one of them a sailor.

Being two Englishmen, it seemed impolite to ask the sort of question often portrayed in stiff upper lip British films, which usually started with, "I say, what the devil do you think you are doing?" Keith was the first to speak when he asked, "Did they just come out of our room?"

"They sure did," I replied. But I never had time to say any more for the door opened again and another couple walked out, even having the effrontery to wish us, "Bon Soir."

In the room while sitting on our beds and trying to decide how to block the through traffic, the inner door opened and yet another couple appeared briefly before disappearing into the hall. It was then we realised our room was the first in a line of three or four, all inter-connected and unless we acted quickly, our sleep was going to be regularly disturbed. The answer was simple. Just lock the outer door, but who had the key? We had both assumed that, as Claude had done the arranging with the 'madame', she must have given him a key. It was only on closer inspection of the door that we found, although there was a keyhole, there was no actual lock!

The alternative was to wedge a chair behind the door, but being a non violent type and having seen the size of some of the sailors, I managed to persuade both of them that discretion would be the better part of valour and if we had to sleep with the blankets over our heads, so be it! From memory I seem to recall some disturbance during the night, but other than sleeping with our valuables under the mattress, the night passed without incident. In the morning Claude claimed that several women had passed through completely naked, but knowing his penchant for exaggeration, it probably meant they were in their bare feet!

Marseilles was certainly an interesting centre of commerce, being the second largest city in France and a major seaport. Out in the bay were a number of islands of historic interest, including the Isle d'If, featured in Alexandre Dumas's 'The Count of Monte Christo'. Claude had never heard of it, Keith had only seen the film and the round trip by boat lasted four hours, so I forgot the idea and added it to my list of things to do before slipping earth's surly bonds. In 2016 it still hovers close to the bottom. We both regretted the meeting being cancelled as there was every indication that a sizeable crowd could have been expected.

When we arrived back at la Sorgue we immediately detected an air of unease amongst the French riders, even Mr Boston was reticent about what had happened. So we found Alberto who told the whole sequence of events the previous day. It seems there had been an argument about those who had served under the Vichy Government which controlled this area of France during world war two. Some people had been deported to Germany to work in factories, while those that stayed led a 'ration free' lifestyle. According to Alberto, Mr Boston was openly accused by the girl friend of one of the riders, which led to fisticuffs and much name calling. How relieved we were that for once they could not malign the English.

Being so close to the end of our tour, we went out of our way to be friendly with everyone. We even spent more time in Mr Boston's office trying to commiserate with him, even asking him about his younger days in Russia. Anything to take away the scowl that we had come to recognise. Perhaps we were also aware that under the agreement, he was to pay our return fares to Dover so that was enough incentive to keep on the right side of him. Two days before the meeting at Isle sur la Sorgue he called all the riders together. This was the first time we had seen the French riders since the fracas and we could not help smiling at one or two bruise marks still visible. Mr Boston began by outlining his deep affection for the town and it's people and how they had seen much hardship during the war. It was his wish that the race promotion could contribute something to the small carnival that was held each year, with proceeds going to help the needy, especially the little children.

Then came the iron fist in the velvet glove. He was prepared to donate a portion of the profits if we would agree to ride for a lower percentage. After such a tear jerking speech, especially the emphasis on the children, no one had the heart to offer any protest, so we all shuffled outside muttering a reluctant agreement. There were no protests from the French team so it seemed that the world war two grievances must have been quietly settled. The one we had nicknamed, 'Desboards' seemed particularly subdued, so perhaps he was the main antagonist.

The council had built a small track as part of the carnival site and although lacking a suitable safety fence, it was going to be adequate for racing. I suspected the other riders were not going to take too many risks and so it proved to be on race day. Had we wanted to, Keith and I could have taken every race, but still practising our 'keep everyone happy' policy, just made it look close. It was only at the interval that we learned everyone had been admitted free anyhow, so there were no takings to share between anyone.

We were now only one meeting away from the journey back to England. It was to be held at Cardenet, another small town down towards Marseilles and was to to be in two days time, the 11th of November. This was a public holiday in France being Armistice Day and it also happened to be Dad's birthday which would be a nice way to round off my season of French speedway. On the day before the meeting, we accompanied Mr Boston to the local railway station where he purchased our return tickets as far as Dover. The bad news was our machines could not travel on the same train and would follow, possibly up to two days later.

There is more right lock on this shot than the camera lens indicates. A low right wrist indicates full bore and I would have liked Eric Langton to have seen this as a tribute to his work. *(Author)*

Yet another battle with Peter Lloyd. Keeping up with him was the hard part. Peter had that lovely crouching style reminiscent of pre-war speedway riders. *(Author)*

Peter Lloyd and me in 2010. Rivals on the 'grass' in the 1950's but still the best of pals.

Another picture to take to my 'Desert Island'. Me on the left and Paul Cross on the right making one of his rapid starts. Tragically, Paul was involved in a fatal accident at a Wetherby grass track in 1965. *(Author)*

CARR CLEANS UP

A large crowd saw Eric Carr (JAP Special) win the East Yorks Centre grass track championship in fine style at Pickering. Runners up were Ken Mellor and Peter Lloyd.

PROVISIONAL RESULTS

250cc: 1 D.Heckle(249 Greeves). 2 E.Shaw(249 DOT). 3 M. Handley (249 Greeves).

350cc TROPHY: 1 P.Lloyd (344 JAP) 2 J.Snowden (344 JAP). 3 K.Mellor (344 JAP).

UNLIMITED TROPHY: 1 P.Lloyd (497 JAP). 2 E. Carr (497 RFP Special). 3 K.Mellor (497 JAP).

E.YORKS CENTRE CHALLENGE: 1 Carr. 2 Mellor. 3 Lloyd.

Inter club prize: Redcar MCC.

A day of honours shared between Eric Carr, Peter Lloyd and me.
(Yorkshire Evening Press)

Clifton Park, Rotherham 1956. George Collinson from Hull on the outside. I'm on the inside. Second from the left is Wilf Green, later to become the UK MZ importer. To accommodate the crowds, the meeting was repeated in the evening. *(Author)*

The photograph that changed my life after it appeared in the Yorkshire Evening Post and was seen by Oliver Langton. This led to being accepted at the Belle Vue Speedway training school. In second place is a life long friend, Dave Giles, who features several times in the book. *(Yorkshire Evening Post)*

The perils of French Speedway. A concrete and iron safety fence! If you were to run a wide bend, not only could you receive serious injuries to yourself, there may be six or more spectators involved. I never did see any disclaimer notices about, 'Motorsport' being dangerous and they were present at their own risk etc. *(Author)*

French Speedway publicity with a quaint of mix of English and French. *(Author)*

A change of name for publicity purposes. Keith Morrison would often sing the lines from the song, 'This could be the start of something big.' It never translated to the foreign riders which proves that humour and songs don't travel well. *(Author)*

Equipe des Coureurs "BOSTON"

Moteur J. A. P., Vitesses Burman, Chaîne Darbilly,
Magnéto M. L. Carburateur Amal, Huile Celor

Victor Boston and troupe 1920s. *(Author)*

Aldershot Stadium 1959 showing the tricky 3rd and 4th bend which visiting riders
could never master. *(John Pilblad)*

First race as Captain of the Aldershot team, June 1960. I am on the outside of my
team mate, Ted Spittles, while Ipswich rider Dennis Day holds the inside line.
(John Pilblad)

(Challenge Match)

BRISTOL: F. Evans 18, C. Julians 12, T.
Usher 3, B. Hughes 3, J. McGill 2, T. Plant
1, C. Francis (res.) 0.

ALDERSHOT: K. Mellor 15, G. Major
12, K. Vale 9, J. Edwards 9, J. Gleed 8,
R. Lambourne 4, K. Prince (res.).

Ht 1: Evans, Mellor, Usher, Lambourne, 67.4. Ht
2: Vale, Major, McGill, Hughes, 70.4. Ht 3: Julians,
Edwards, Gleed, Plant, 70.6. Ht 4: Mellor, Lam-
bourne, McGill, Hughes (f), 68.8. Ht 5: Major,
Julians, Vale, Plant, 69.4. Ht 6: Evans, Gleed,
Edwards, Usher, 68.6. Ht 7: Mellor, Julians, Plant,
Lambourne, 69.2. Ht 8: Evans, Major, Vale, Usher,
67. Ht 9: Julians, Gleed, Edwards, Francis, 70.4. Ht
10: Evans, Mellor, Vale, McGill, 67.8. Ht 11: Major,
Hughes, Gleed, Julians (f), 69.8. Ht 12: Edwards,
Usher, Lambourne, Plant, 71.4. Ht 13: Vale, Mellor,
Hughes, Julians (f), 71. Ht 14: Evans, Edwards,
Lambourne, McGill. 70.2. Ht 15: Evans, Major,
Gleed, McGill, 68.6. Ht 16: Mellor, Julians, Gleed,
Evans (f), 69.

TOP FOUR KNOCK OUT: Ht 1: Evans, Julians,
Francis, McGill, 67.8. Ht 2: Mellor, Vale, Edwards,
Major, 70.4. Final: Evans, Mellor, Julians, Vale, 68.4.

A high scoring meeting and my first visit to the Bristol track. The performance was
noted by the Bristol management. *(Speedway Star)*

Diving into the first bend at Southampton in front of 6000 people. Partially obscured on my left is team mate, Peter Vandenberg and holding the inside line is Colin Goody (Ipswich) Len Silver is at the rear. *(Cecil Bailey)*

Did I ever tell you about me being an 'All Star?' *(Author)*

Our mileage was nearer 1000 due to taking various detours from the recommended route to admire the scenery. On the left, Ken Boulter with his 1936 250cc Ariel Red Hunter. John Guppy with his 1931 Ariel Model B and my BSA B44 Victor. It was a trouble free journey apart from John making an adjustment to the primary chain. *(Author)*

222 years of Mellor family sitting on Flamborough Head. If I was ever invited to take part in 'Desert island Discs', this would be one of the luxury items I would take with me. *(Author)*

Dad with his DKW 'Hummel' (Bumblebee). He was nearing the end of his riding years and had already indicated that he would stop when the new helmet legislation came into force. But he did a credible amount of mileage on the February, 1955 registered machine. It was 49cc and featured 3-speed drive. *(Author)*

The year is 1983 and it may have been the last time Dad sat astride a motorcycle with the engine running. He really fancied a potter around the car park and it was only the intervention of mum that persuaded him otherwise. Nevertheless, he remained keen and alert, still able to recall many events from his younger years right to the end of his days. He died in 1992. *(Author)*

Skaw Bay on the Isle of Unst. The most northerly part of the British Isles by road. The Norton in front of my BMW belonged to Joe Gray, secretary of the Shetland Motorcycle Club. *(Author)*

Team M20 at a Midlands Rally. On the right is Gordon Jeal's GOB 108 which left the factory on 20 August, 1945, some 3 years before mine. Please note the matching helmets. *(Author)*

1951 BSA B31 found in a cellar and restored by Hughie Hancox, better known for his Triumph expertise. *(Author)*

Leaving the pits on my return to speedway racing in the vintage league after a 35 year lay off! It was just another 'moment of truth'. *(Author)*

Happy days amongst the veterans at Poole speedway. Bill Holden on the machine had ridden for them in 1952 and was 72 at the time of the photo. Next to me on the extreme left is Ross Gilberton who started with me at Aldershot.
(*Bournemouth Evening Echo*)

The day I won a Silver Medal at the Banbury Run.

The 'Yorkie' Bar Kid in the Banbury Run, 2010. On my way to winning a Silver Medal.
(Peter Wileman)

1929 500cc York. Built in Coventry in the old Omega factory for Robert Sturm of
Vienna. In vintage circles it may be 'cheap and cheerful', but it has romped up Sun
Rising Hill three times. In addition to mine, there are 8 other survivors, all in Austria.
(Photography by Michael Rothwell)

1937 BSA M20, the year of manufacture and the Warwickshire registration number indicates the month February. For reasons mentioned in the text, if I had to select one machine from my collection I would have to pick this one.
(Photography by Michael Rothwell)

1946 BSA C11 250cc. Grey porridge in many motorcyclists opinions, but you'd be surprised how many people come up and say, "I had one of those."
(Photography by Michael Rothwell)

1969 BSA B44 (441cc). Finished in the factory colour Peony red. It has covered over 20,000 miles in my care, including a trip from John O'Groats to Lands End in 1994. *(Photography by Michael Rothwell)*

1970 BSA 'Basuki'. Based on the B25 model, but fitted with a Susuki GN250 engine. It is my secret weapon against the ageing motorcyclists problem of kick starting on a winter morning. Fitted with electric start, 5 gears and 4-valve head it has transformed the machine. Such a pity that Small Heath did not think about it 50 years earlier. *(Photography by Michael Rothwell)*

The closest I shall probably come to motorcycling luxury. My 1982 BMW R65, now with 61,000 miles to its credit. I have contributed nearly 40,000 of them, and in that time, the cylinder heads have not been removed.
(Photography by Michael Rothwell)

Uncle Joe Mellor remembered high on the memorial at Thiepval, along with 72,000 others that have no known grave to their sacrifices between 1914 and 1918.

On the final night of business, Dad back in the operating box at the Tower cinema, Leeds, 6 March 1985. He opened the cinema in 1920 and knocked out the projector porthole behind him. *(Yorkshire Evening Post)*

In the evening we decided to make our presentation to Alberto and began gathering our engine spares together. We wanted to do it between the three of us without the knowledge of anyone, especially Claude, so just before the evening meal we managed to lure him out of the hotel on the pretext of checking our machines. We had found a suitable flat box in which we placed the surplus piston rings, valves and springs, sparking plugs and spare HT lead, plus a selection of carburettor spares. It was a touching moment when he opened it and he was truly overcome by our gesture. It was one of those moments when words seemed superfluous as he beamed with pleasure and placed his arms around our shoulders conveying his appreciation in a mixture of Spanish and English.

The journey to Cardenet by way of country roads was about thirty miles and Mr Boston and Claude made an early start. The meeting was yet another tie up with the local sports club which meant nothing could be relied upon to have been completed. The track had originally been used for athletics but was now disused. We knew this would mean the usual style of concrete posts and iron leaning rail around the outside. For our final appearance in France, Alberto was to take us in his Citroen, a welcome relief from the comedy duo of father and son driving the lorry with an almost running commentary of sarcastic banter as to correct gear or correct throttle opening.

As we changed into our leathers for the last time, there was a slight feeling of regret. We had perhaps lapsed a little too cosily into the barn storming life of French speedway. May be we were entertaining crowds by racing a speedway machine around an oval track. Then of course there was the publicity we had achieved in the European columns of the speedway press. We were still responsible for sending the reports from France, therefore we made sure the copy was suitably 'biased' in our favour. But our original ambition was to break into British speedway and this was still some way into the future.

For our final appearance in France, we made sure we provided the crowd with plenty of displays of broad siding. It wouldn't have won many races in England, but it raised a few gasps from the terraces. And for the final race, we did our usual party piece of coming through the leading pair on the last bend of the last lap. As we touched hands in acknowledgement, for the first time in six months we actually received applause from the crowd. The local beauty queen presented all the riders with a bottle of

Champagne, provided by one of the local cafes and heavily 'plugged' over the loudspeaker. We later learned that we all had to appear there after the meeting which wasn't the ordeal we at first imagined. Especially as Keith and I were the centre of attention from around forty school girls who were in their final year of English and wanted to know, amongst many other things, if we had seen the Queen, Prime Minister Harold Macmillan, Tommy Steele, Cliff Richard and Frankie Vaughan.

Wednesday, the day of departure was something of an anti-climax. Alberto had already bid us farewell after the meeting. He was heading straight back to Spain to take over a vehicle repair shop. The other riders, particularly the French, seemed to have disappeared during the night. While we never expected any gushing farewells, we were perhaps thinking of a handshake and a cheery wave. For the rest of the day we prepared our machines for the journey. First removing the rear chain then securing it to the saddle, still in it's well greased state as a deterrent to anyone who might think of 'trying it for size'. We had retained all labels and tags and other than changing the destination and locking the clutch lever and twist grip, we delivered them to the station. Once again with a sinking feeling that once we departed, everything else had to be left to the railway's efficiency.

We said all our farewells at the old house which we now assumed would be the Boston's winter quarters. As the last hours ticked away, Mr Boston kept us amused with another selection of his 'risque' army jokes from his days in India. His tales of the Raj may have been amusing if he had not tried to imitate the dialect. Unfortunately, his thick Russian guttural accent did little to convey any humour in the stories. As a final gesture he made us a cup of tea, making a great show of crooking his little finger in the well mannered style of colonels and their mem-sahibs he claimed to have entertained some thirty five years earlier. He could even sing a few opening lines to some of the songs to which the army had adapted their own lyrics to. 'Kiss me goodnight sergeant major' and 'I wouldn't leave my little wooden hut for you' were just two which passed an hour until train time. Claude, who had been unusually quiet, joined in an occasional chorus. He had probably heard them all since his childhood.

Neither of them wanted to join us on the platform. Mr Boston had allowed his scowl to soften a little as he wished us Bon Nuit and a safe journey. There was genuine emotion as he shook our hands and hoped we had success in our quest for speedway fame. He asked if we would write and let him know about our progress, even asking if we would try and find some riders for the following year. As for Claude, it seemed the parting was too much for him and we were given a quick handshake before he dashed out of the door.

We were the only passengers waiting on the platform. A faint light was showing from an office alongside the goods shed where we presumed our machines were awaiting transit. It seemed an unlikely stopping place for a train from Marseilles to Paris, but our tickets clearly stated a through journey with no changes so we waited.

A few minutes before 7pm a bell sounded and a train appeared out of the gloom. One thing I had to credit the French with was the apparent efficiency and punctuality of their railways. We climbed into the first available compartment, struggling with our luggage. We both had a military kit bag containing our racing leathers and helmet, plus a tool box each, all of which was observed with a little trepidation by two matronly looking ladies in the compartment.

No words had been spoken and we settled down to a long overnight journey. Before long one of them hissed a warning to her companion, asking, "Do you think we are going to be safe, Millicent?"

Keith had already adopted a dozing position and as I made no indication that I had understood the question, she continued,

"You know what Frenchmen are. I think they are sailors."

Her companion replied with a trace of anxiety,

"Oh! Emily. don't be so melodramatic. They are probably going home on leave to see their loved ones."

By now I was trying hard to curb my amusement and knowing Keith was only feigning sleep, he too must have been close to laughter. My warped sense of humour wanted to say something astonishing such as, "Hello Darling, fancy a good time?.

It was only the thought that they may have acted drastically by pulling the communication cord, that persuaded me to continue with an air of ignorance. Then Emily, with a little bravado said,

"The one on your side has nice features. He reminds me of Trevor Howard."

Millicent, who now must have been convinced it was safe to speak added,

"Did you see him in 'Brief Encounter? Wasn't he gorgeous. Oh! If only it really was him."

They soon tired of their fantasising but not before they had pledged to stay awake and if one of them were to start to feel sleepy, the other had to rouse them. By the time the train arrived at Dijon, it was well past midnight. Nevertheless, the two ladies were still alert with their paperback novels firmly in their grasp.

As we neared Orly, the station for the airport, the ladies began to gather their belongings. I decided this was the time to act. Nudging Keith, I rose and said,

"Can we help you with your luggage?" Bye the way, we are not sailors, we're a couple of speedway riders heading for Calais and England."

The look of shock on both their faces was a picture of embarrassment and maidenly blushes. Keith added, "He looks nothing like Trevor Howard. More like Frankie Howerd!"

As the train pulled out, they remained starring at the ground, not risking any eye contact with our two grinning faces at the window.

Changing stations in Paris and travelling by the Metro system was going to be easier than when we first arrived. This time we were earlier than most workers so the complaints about excess luggage were few. We were even in luck when we arrived at Gare du Nord, a train for Calais was waiting to leave and we were soon speeding through the environs of Paris and out into the countryside towards a ferry for Dover.

At Calais we had some difficulty trying to explain that there were two racing motorcycles to follow and payment was included in our tickets. Showing the Customs paperwork did help but we were hampered by not understanding the questions we were being asked. We were saved by an elderly couple who offered to help and we soon had everything completed. They were intrigued when they heard what we had been doing for the last six months and when they mentioned they ran a small bed and breakfast guest house in Dover and had a room vacant which would allow us to await the arrival of the machines, our problems were over. Or so we thought.

Our first night in England for six months followed by a full English breakfast was a tremendous boost to our flagging morale. It prepared us for the disappointing news that our machines would not arrive in Dover until Monday, three days hence. This left the only option to return to

Leeds, collect my vehicle and set off back early on Monday morning. This seemed a safer alternative than allowing British Railways to convey them. True they had already travelled both ways across France, but that ever present statistic, 'the law of averages' does have an uncanny way of turning up on every third turn of a card. It was a simple case of hedging one's bets. To ease our burden, Val and Harry, who ran the guest house, suggested we leave our luggage with them and collect it on our return. It certainly made the return railway journey to Leeds more pleasurable.

We were back in Dover by mid afternoon the following Monday and over joyed to find our machines were ready to be collected. In the meantime, I had been in contact with the team manager of Aldershot Speedway and informed him of my arrival back in England. I also mentioned that, as I was in Dover on the Monday, if it was convenient for him, I could travel up to Aldershot and meet him at the stadium the next day. Keith was happy to drive my pick up back to Leeds and unload everything.

Val and Harry had a vacancy. In fact they had three as it was now out of season, so I joined them for dinner and an evening of television, along with breakfast before leaving. As I journeyed by train through the 'Garden of England', I was forming a mental picture of a speedway promoter along with his team manager. I knew it was not going to be Wembley Stadium but I conjured up a vision of someone in a dark brown suit, sitting behind a leather topped desk, surrounded by a battery of telephones. A long legged secretary would come in and ask if I would like tea or coffee. To say the reverie was shattered would be an understatement of vast proportions.

I started walking from the railway station, following directions from a local shopkeeper who said it would take no more than ten minutes. As I neared the right turn into Oxenden Road, my imagination was setting me down gently for the initial shock. There was no huge grandstand to be seen, no office block incorporating turnstiles and no high perimeter fence. Not even a sign saying Aldershot Stadium. I had arrived at a rough patch of ground which served as the car park, beyond which was a fence that may or may not have been secure. The concrete posts which had once been upright, now pointed at various angles while still attempting to support the chain link netting.

An iron framed gate was half open and beyond a man was painting some white boards. Clearing my throat as a friendly opener, I asked him where I could find the speedway promoter.

"He's probably on the track," he replied in an amiable voice. Where else I thought. I expect he's supervising some refurbishment of equipment or maybe over-seeing preparations of the track surface. I continued inside and crossed over the greyhound track, where I had my first real glimpse of what had been a third division speedway track. Was this really going to reopen? Out on the track I could see someone on their knees with an arm down a drain.

"I'm looking for Mr John Pilblad."

"That's me!" he laughed as he retrieved a handful of slurry from the drain. I realised there was no chance of a welcoming handshake!

"Let me finish here then we'll go over to the clubhouse, there's some tea on."

Ah I thought, that must be where the leather topped desk is, maybe the long legged secretary too. I was wrong on both counts. Already my illusion was fading. I began to think there was little difference from what I had left in France. Only here the tracks were permanent, featured lighting all the way around and everyone spoke English.

Five minutes later he joined me after removing most of the mud.

"Fancy some tea?" he said.

Surely I thought, this isn't where the secretary appears. It wasn't. He handed me a kettle, saying, fill this while I find some cups.

By now there was no trace of my illusion. We were joined by Ted Payne, the team manager and the desk became a Formica topped table.

"Are you interested in signing for us?" he asked. "If so, is your racing licence up to date and are you prepared to move to the south of England."

It was all happening too quickly for me. Was this the real world of speedway? If so was I really on the verge of becoming a professional speedway rider. Without thinking I answered yes to all three questions. I signed a contract form, which I never saw again, added two sugars to my tea and tried to take it all in. I don't even remember walking back to the railway station, in fact I remember little of the entire journey back to Leeds, such was the feeling of euphoria.

The remaining weeks of 1958 were almost a blur. There was much planning and organising to be completed and it was now that my contacts with the other English riders I had met in France was beneficial. My first call was to George Bason who was to prove invaluable in arranging, not only accommodation, but employment that would provide an income for the start of the new year. George lived at Marlow and had in fact ridden at Aldershot back in 1952, so at least he could provide me with inside information about the track.

1959 started with some of the worst snowstorms Britain had seen for years. Transport, both road and rail was badly affected, with the result I had to delay my move south until mid January. Sadly, the day I arrived coincided with the death of World Motor Racing Champion, Mike Hawthorn, due to a road accident only a mile from Aldershot Stadium.

George helped me to settle in and took me to meet a number of riders in the area. Most of them I knew by name, but within the next few months I would be coming up to the starting line with many of them. With the prospect of Aldershot reopening and the formation of a new Southern Area League, an appeal went out for volunteers to help with a number of tasks to ensure the track would be ready for the new season. Not only that, there were many facilities that needed to be in place to make certain a racing licence would be granted by the Speedway Control Board.

The weekend work teams did a fine job, not only re-establishing the track, but installing lighting and safety features that had to be provided for the safety of the public. I was also given some guidance by George Bason. He began riding on speedway in the thirties and had done the rounds of a number of tracks from Liverpool to Southampton. He saw no harm in creating publicity features for the magazines if it meant a photograph or a mention in their columns, which is why he suggested I joined the Speedway X1 football team which played charity matches against show business and sporting teams. He was right too, for it resulted in several photographs and column inches and it usually linked my name with Aldershot.

George also ran a motorcycle repair shop and agreed to take my machine in for pre-season preparation. The months in France had not been too demanding on the engine, but with only two months to the start of a new season and in view of the poor quality French fuel, it was time for some internal work. There were also practice laps required after some of the indifferent French tracks.

The main training track in England was at Rye House in Hertfordshire, which had first opened in 1935 and over the years has become renowned for unearthing many talented youngsters who progressed to mainstream speedway. George had ridden there before the second war, when it was licensed under the Sunday Dirt Track League and as he knew the way, was willing to accompany me. Rye House were also entering a team in the new league.

It paid off too, for after three or four sessions, He mentioned my name to Freddy Millward, who was team manager and although I was not available for the team, he suggested I came along for their first home Sunday meeting and take a place in the second half events. Although too late for inclusion in the printed programme, I was given two rides and scored three points with a satisfying second and third place.

Even more pleasurable was meeting up with Derek Timms, who had already been signed by Aldershot and with whom I would share many races as team members. Derek's career had started in the early fifties at a number of midland tracks, which sadly all folded with the later decline of speedway. Due to untold administrative difficulties with the Speedway Control Board, the Aldershot track was not ready for the start of the season, with the result all the first fixtures were completed at 'away' tracks. Nevertheless, the first time I donned an Aldershot race jacket with the target emblem, hence the nickname 'Shots', I couldn't help remembering it was close to ten years since I had first plucked up courage to ask Oliver Langton, 'How do I become a speedway rider?' I did warn in earlier pages that my story was not one of overnight success!

The opening at Tongham Stadium went well and received good publicity in the magazines. The speedway press now seemed to be using Tongham Stadium when referring to Aldershot, it being the name of the nearby village. However, Tongham was over the boundary in Surrey, whereas, Aldershot was firmly rooted in Hampshire. But it didn't stop them from using such headlines as, 'This week Aldershot entertain Bristol at the Surrey raceway.'

Everyone went home satisfied. Even the race referee was able to forward his Control Board report form with no blemishes. But riders were not happy with the track. Not the surface but the shape. The track was not a perfect oval, but in the shape of a kite, with bends one and two fast and very ridable, while bends three and four could not be ridden in the conventional style. The effect was, if you were leading the race into the third bend on the last lap, you were almost a certain winner. Strangely, I never found it daunting and I have always put it down to my years on Yorkshire grass tracks, where you just accepted what you were confronted with.

Aldershot had started with a solid team, but as the resurgence in speedway grew, riders such as Derek Timms, Peter Vandenberg and Ross Gilbertson were poached by the National League teams. But there was still a solid core for team manager, Ted Payne, to make his weekly selection. Such as, Ken Vale, George Major, Bill Osborne, John Edwards and (hopefully) the author.

Looking back on the period after a lapse of fifty plus years, it seemed to pass quickly and the close season was around again. Nevertheless, it was very satisfying and that teenage ambition was now complete. What I was not to realise during the winter months prior to the 1960 season, there was to be one more accolade.

Motorcycle road mileage had lapsed during the racing season. Not only from lack of available time, but from having no access to a machine. This was remedied when I met someone who followed speedway, but preferred to take an active part in trials in the winter months. He owned a Greeves for competition work and a BSA B31 (what else!) for road use. As he always opted to use the Greeves, I could have access to the BSA whenever I wished.

Exploring the lanes of Buckinghamshire became a very enjoyable period and, following me paying for new tyres, chains and a battery, even a couple of trips to Yorkshire, involving round trip mileages that I have seldom exceeded since. The BSA B31 was an ideal machine for use as an occasional 'hack' and when it came up for sale, I was tempted to buy it. Then my colleague died very suddenly and the machine became part of his estate, which was disposed of by his family with seemingly inordinate haste.

Prior to the start of the 1960 season, along with several other team members, I took the opportunity of several sessions at Rye House just to shake off the winter blues and to ensure the machine was set-up correctly. The one drawback with a speedway machine was, after carrying out various adjustments, you could not take it up the road for a 'spin'.

The formation of the Southern Area League was now being taken seriously, even if there were some who likened it to the old third division of the early fifties with non of the glamour of the higher divisions. But it had it's supporters and was able to provide entertaining racing in a fun style at a lower cost, which was one of the contributing factors to the formation. We were now entering that period soon to be dubbed, 'swinging sixties' and without doubt, speedway saw a rise in popularity during these years. But there were some who regarded it as a period of unrestrained recklessness and degradation. You paid your money and you took your choice. For me, my eye was still firmly fixed on ambition.

As I took my place in the team for the start of the new season, little was I to know of a number of changes that the next six months were to bring. The most significant change was to lead me into a new career which lasted until close to the end of the old century. But until then there was still time to enjoy the publicity that the speedway magazines would pump out every week. Their journalistic licence was often based on the theory of, 'why lose a good story for the sake of a few facts! Nevertheless, the fans seemed to enjoy it and even if I was a small fish in a small pond, I had finally made it to the other side of the safety fence from where my first ambitions had begun some eleven years earlier.

Autographs and adoration were all part of the scene and you went along with the flow. Some called it a cheap and sensational sport based on nothing more than teen-age hysteria, but once the starting tapes had gone up more dignities could be lowered in the space of two minutes than anywhere else. But it was a team sport and you were out to win against rival opposition, a situation that would be frequently pointed out by the team manager if the points tally was not in our favour. The renaissance of old tracks during the winter months began to provide more opportunities for extra rides in addition to the league fixtures and for one meeting at Bristol my points tally gave me my first paid maximum and the resulting magazine publicity did not go unnoticed.

At the time, Bill Osborne was team captain but was being troubled by an old injury and requested that he stood down enabling him to move to the reserve berth. The promoter and team manager seemed to be of the opinion that I was a worthy replacement and so for the match versus Ipswich on June 18 I took over the number one position. It probably passed unnoticed to many supporters but for me it was a personal achievement that made my original ambition complete. But we were only half way through the season, when I was called into the office and told that I was to be transferred to Southampton in the National League. The same promotion company owned Bristol Speedway and it seemed my performance there had been noted.

To use a simple football team analogy, it was like going from Scunthorpe United to Manchester United and it was not an easy change to make.

Being in the first division of speedway meant the costs were higher, even though the points money and travelling expenses kept pace with the rising maintenance needed. Although I had no say in the contract, one clause I was grateful for enabled me to still ride for Aldershot if I was not required by the Southampton management. It was one of these occasions that gave me one of my greatest satisfactions in speedway and the circumstances that brought it about were the butt of much ribbing for a good number of years after.

Bristol were booked to ride at Aldershot and by coincidence, their captain was Trevor Redmond, a New Zealander, who had ridden for the 'Shots' between 1950 and 1952 and had been nigh unbeatable around the Tongham track. In the years following the war, many motorcyclists, and certainly speedway riders, favoured the ex-army gas goggles that were 'two a penny' on the army surplus market. In fact they were so cheap you could dispose of them after one race and all that held them in place was a simple length of elastic. In the standard programme formula of speedway racing, the captains meet in the first heat and Trevor was no doubt eager to come to the tapes, having already been well eulogised by the announcer. In crowd terms, many former supporters had come along to see him and it proved to be the biggest crowd of the season.

I was already late leaving the pits and as I pulled the goggles over the peak of my helmet, the elastic broke, leaving me with no eye protection. I had drawn the inside position with Trevor on my right and as I drew up to the tapes, it was not unnatural for him to look to his left to see the opposition. I noticed him look then do a double take as he saw I was wearing no goggles, but that was his failing for up went the tapes and I was away, gaining that all important lead into the first bend. For four laps he tried everything to pass me, but by the time I saw the yellow last lap flag I knew the race was mine. Nothing was said back in the pits, although I did hear later from a marshal that he made some derogatory remark about 'that cocky young *******'.

As the 1960 season moved into September I was reaching a stage in life where a decision had to be made. The crowd attendance at Aldershot had not come up to the expectations of the promoters in so far as covering week to week running expenses. Added to this, the continuing resurgence of speedway and the reopening of old venues to form a new Provincial League brought pressure from the Southampton management for me to re-sign for the new season with an arrangement whereby I would be loaned out to their joint promotion at Bristol. All of this had to be considered against my growing interest in sound recording following a meeting with someone who had a machine that could produce 78rpm records from a tape recorder. Little did I know then that as I soldered cables, spliced recording tape and built various audio kits in his attic bed sitter in Tooting, that it was to lead to a whole new life for the next forty years. Perhaps the greatest factor in making the decision was the awareness that I had competed for three seasons without sustaining any injuries and knowing that the 'Law of Averages', that mythical belief that events or happenings, however small, must effect the outcome across a large proportion of the population. I was not prepared to tempt fate.

I may not have been wholly convinced at the time but many years later it was put to me in a more plausible variant by a former rear gunner in a Halifax bomber, who had survived forty missions over enemy territory. He dismissed such words as luck or fate and summed it up as just one of life's percentages. We have not strayed too far away from the theme of motorcycles because my colleague in the attic bedsitter who was called Alan, had a Vespa scooter fitted with a sidecar. Alan had no knowledge of internal combustion engines or what was required to keep them running. He would hold a spanner as if it were a fountain pen. But give him a pile of resistors, coils, capacitors and a soldering iron, he could knock up a radio in five minutes. My contact with the scooter world was brief and I only rode it three or four times. The handling was frightening so what it would have been like as a solo, I shudder to imagine. All I did was to keep it running in return for a substantial meal once a week. Alan's other talent was being able to produce homely cooking from a single electric cooker ring.

The little 250cc BSA had seen little use for the past year. Dad had now purchased a DKW 'Hummel' which he delighted in telling everyone, meant bumble bee. I found it certainly 'buzzed' along the first time I took it out and as it had reasonable brakes, was certainly equal to the NSU 'Quickly'. He had now joined a company that owned seven cinemas in the Leeds area which meant he could be called upon at short notice to run the show at any one of them, to cover for illness or holiday breaks, so the DKW was the ideal machine. In the last five years before retirement, he covered close to 12000 miles with only the usual replacements such as tyres, chain, plugs, bulbs and cables being required. After retirement his mileage was confined to his local district as he had become convinced that traffic was now much closer to him.

At the first opportunity I gave the BSA a major service, even replacing the clevis pins in the hand change mechanism. The performance was what you would expect for a 1936 250cc and the first outing was a real trip down memory lane as I travelled along many of the roads I had first covered thirteen years earlier. Subsequent trips tended to be around the same route and as there was no speedo mileage trip, I had no indication of distance. It was only after covering the route by car that I was pleasantly surprised to find it was 43 miles. The little machine took it in it's stride. Just what the total mileage was I had no idea, but it had no undue rattles and was using little oil with no visible trace of blue smoke from the exhaust, so it was a case of that old saying, "If it ain't broke, don't fix it."

Being steeped in a cinema background from early childhood gave me a deluded belief that gaining entry to the film industry would be just a formality. How little I knew about the power of the trade union movement in Britain. In reality it was a 'closed shop' policy, where you could only get a job if you had a union ticket and you could only get a union ticket if you had a job. Alan said it could take years so why not throw my lot in with him and learn the recording business the hard way.

Most of his location work involved choirs or church services, usually reached on his Vespa outfit. I drew the line at riding on the pillion and bought myself a BMW Isetta bubble car which could easily outpace the Vespa and proved to be a real fun vehicle, even making several trips to Yorkshire.

With Alan providing some income in addition to supplementary work as an auto electrician those early months of 1961 passed without too much anguish. I had sold my speedway machine at a virtual 'giveaway' price to a young hopeful, although I was still receiving persuasive letters from Southampton promoter Charlie Knott, asking if I would reconsider my decision to retire from racing. It was all very tempting, especially when he offered to provide a machine that could be maintained in the stadium workshop. But at the age of 27 even I was brave enough to admit that the remaining racing years would not be easy. This was brought home to me when I attended a session at Rye House to watch some of the new teenage riders putting in some practice laps. Youth was not on my side.

I came to know more about Alan as we spent more working hours together. He had a quirky sense of humour, rather in the style of Alan Bennett and he was a good raconteur. It was usually after the Friday night feast that he would go off into a long monologue spiced with twists of humour. I discovered that the Vespa was not his first form of powered transport. In 1949 he had bought one of the first cycle clip-on Mini Motor power units which were made in Croydon. He passed his test on this, then graduated to a Raynel auto cycle before moving up market (his expression) to the Vespa.

One Friday night after he had finished off the sherry trifle, he told me a story that had me in stitches until he confessed he was the one responsible and it had cost him his job. He had worked for the BBC World Service and was in charge of news broadcasts to overseas countries in the appropriate language. One night while loading a tape recorder with a reel of news in Arabic, he had failed to notice that it had not been rewound to the start and when transmission time came, he pressed the start button and broadcast the news running backwards to three north African countries. Apparently, it sounded more or less the same on the monitor speaker and it continued for five minutes before the phone lines at Bush House in London were jammed with irate listeners in Morocco, Tunisia and Algeria.

When I related the story to Dad on my next visit to Yorkshire, he too found it hilarious. He had a fund of stories from his years in the cinema operating box and I know he added Alan's mishap to them. I did, however, regret for a long time afterwards, my lack of sensitivity when he first told me about his fall from broadcasting prestige. But to his credit, he went on to develop a growing business in location sound, whereby events, public functions and performances could be recorded and made available on limited number disc records.

For me this meant more mileage in the Isetta and I had to seriously consider moving to four wheels. I had made my last payment on the bubble car so weekly finances were easing, but affording that extra wheel was almost a bridge too far. One trip to the midlands turned into a journey of epic proportions. Returning down the A1 near Stamford, the cylinder head gasket blew causing a total loss of power. I was carrying a good selection of tools and soon had the head off where I found that the alloy had also distorted. I walked into Stamford, caught a bus to Peterborough, then a train to King's Cross and went straight to Godfrey's in Great Portland Street, the Isetta agents, where I purchased a replacement head and the necessary gaskets.

Then it was back to the flat for a good nights rest before retracing the journey back to the lay-by on the Stamford bypass. Within a couple of hours the engine was ready to run and as I was replacing the fan cowling, a lorry pulled in and the driver came over to see if he could help in any way. He told me he had seen me the day before as he was heading north and was surprised to find me still in the lay-by on his return from Arbroath!

Alan and I had purchased high quality portable tape recorders and following the publication of Doctor Beeching's plan to scrap the steam locomotive from Britain's railways, began to find a demand from enthusiasts for recordings. One of these just happened to be a car salesman for a chain of garages in south London and he was able to obtain cars taken in part exchange but too old for the forecourt, at a very low price. So for a deposit of £2 I secured a 1954 Morris Minor, leaving a balance to pay of £53. It was even a genuine 'one lady owner', a district nurse in fact, so it had led a sedate life.

This was to change only two months later when it was stolen during the night(Friday the 13th). Worse still, it was due to go for the MOT test and in preparation I had left the log book and old certificate in the glove box! Four weeks later (now into 1964) I received a phone call from Buckinghamshire Police, stating the car had been recovered after a lady had bought it for £70 then tried to renew the road fund licence. The end result was, I recovered the vehicle, she lost her money and the thief was jailed for six months, but the Minor continued to give good service for many more miles.

Alan had also moved on. He had purchased an Austin Mini, which I collected for him. I even gave him some basic driving tuition on the car park of nearby Wimbledon Speedway stadium. Once again his prowess came to the fore with a first time pass when he applied to take the driving test.

Motorcycles may appear to have taken a back seat during this period, but I kept in touch with a close colleague who was forging a name for himself on Yorkshire grass tracks and even further afield such as Lincolnshire, Derbyshire and Cambridgeshire. The Isetta had taken me to a good number of meetings and this increased when I acquired the

'Moggy Minor'. I also attended several vintage events, including the start of a number of London to Brighton runs. It was at one of these that I first came to know Owen Tyler and his Scott; LK2507. Built in Yorkshire but registered in London. It was originally the prized possession of a soldier in the first war, who like thousands more, never returned.

Once again that fickle hand of fate, coincidence, or what ever term you wish to choose played it's card. Almost thirty years later, after I had joined the Association of Pioneer Motorcyclists, later becoming the last newsletter editor of the old century, Owen and I would meet at lunches or at gatherings for veterans. I can still recall his delightful banter, as I could when I wrote his obituary in 1998.

Still trying to gain a foothold in the film industry, I signed up to attend a film school course in sound recording which involved two nights each week for a period of four months. My applications for union membership were still falling on stoney ground and even if I was not taking work from members, by the time I could show proof of this the opportunity had passed. Alan's work had moved into other areas of sound, such as public address systems that could be hired to events organisers or copying tapes for two prominent London psychologists. Monitoring the content could be mind numbing and I could never understand how patients were expected to recover after listening to an hour's programme. But I always looked forward to delivering the orders as both doctors would instruct their Spanish maids to prepare some delightful junket in their lavish Mayfair kitchens.

I had not completely shunned speedway racing and attended a number of meetings, not only in the London area, but in the midlands and the north. The new Provincial League with an entirely different breed of promoters had shaken the old Control Board into submission and the old die-hards, many dating from pre-war days had to accept changes. Seeing racing from the terraces again brought no yearning to go back. To use a more modern expression, I had been there, done that and got the T-shirt.

But later pages will show, thirty years later in fact when vintage speedway racing became a popular attraction in second half events at modern meetings, the urge to 'have a go' became a reality. The fact that I finally made the grade into the film industry, and later television does not really have a place in this story, other than to mention any direct or indirect connection to motorcycles. One of these occurred when I met a fellow sound recordist, Les Brumpton, in 1964. Not only did we share a preoccupation in recording sound but also a fondness for the cinema organ and fairground organ. For the next twenty years we amassed a huge collection of master tapes of which a good number were issued as LPs and later cassettes and CDs. But Les was also a motorcyclist, having a Triumph T120 when I first came to know him. But in his twenties he had been a real speed demon with machines ranging from a Vincent Black Shadow, Norton International, BSA Rocket Gold Star, Velocette Venom and a BMW R69. In his garage he also had an Ariel WNG in very original army trim. Whenever I paid a visit to his Lincolnshire home I would take it out for a spin around the flat fenland roads. It was obviously no match for the T120 and Les was always out of sight before I reached the end of his drive.

One occasion on the way back from Skegness, we had swapped machines and Les was pushing the Ariel at his usual wide open throttle position when the magneto points became loose with the consequent loss of a spark. We still had around fifteen miles to travel and in our roadside haste we lost the fibre tappet that opens the face cam points. In a 'get you home' style of bodge, we made a replacement from a piece of hawthorn twig, as a temporary measure Les assured me, but I rode the machine at least a dozen times afterwards and found it to be an easy starter with our 'mod'. Les turned to high performance cars later, but he sold the Ariel to a local farmer as a runner and it continued to give good service. Owners of Fireblades, Bandits, Virages etc may marvel at modern technology, but if it goes wrong in the middle of nowhere you just have to hope that you are within mobile phone range.

3:   1967 to 1990

As we left the 'swinging sixties' and entered the 'seventies', these were to be my lean years for motorcycling. For the past six years or so Les and I had worked on a variety of programmes for film and television, both in Britain and overseas with an attitude of take anything so long as it pays the rent. Even visits to Dad and Mum were often in and out on the way to or from locations. Whenever possible I started the 250cc BSA just for the satisfaction of hearing the familiar purr of the exhaust and chatter of the open valve gear. Dad was now enjoying a well earned retirement but was reluctant to take the BSA out. He had already indicated that the forthcoming legislation regarding the wearing of crash helmets would bring an end to his riding days. But he still enjoyed the DKW and the quiet suburban streets of north Leeds were the perfect location for him to recapture all those past years on two wheels. It also enabled me to log a few more miles. The advantage being you could ride it just as you were dressed and it was to be the last machine I rode before the 1973 Helmet Law.

One subject he had always puzzled over from his motorcycle years was chain drive. He always maintained that the belt drive was much smoother than chain (how he would chuckle if he knew that some of todays super bikes boasted belt drive). He also thought manufacturers stayed too long with chain as opposed to shaft drive. I had my first encounter with shaft drive in 1976 when Les rang to tell me he had bought a BMW R100/7 which also featured a front disc brake.

My first outing was very impressive, despite the strange effect of a flat twin after years of handling British singles. I reported back to Dad confirming he was right about shaft drive transmission, but it was to be seventeen years before I finally acquired a BMW. Sadly too late for him to witness. 1976 was a year of sadness. Not for the passing of family or friends, but a situation that arose regarding the disposal of the little 250cc BSA along with the DKW 'Hummel'. It just so happened that I was away on a long location assignment and was unable to be contacted for a decision. A family friend told Dad that his son was starting college and needed some transport that would not cost too much to run. In a moment of hastiness Dad agreed to let them have both machines if it would help the situation and I never did find out how much he was paid. The outcome was, the father rode the DKW and the son pushed the BSA across Leeds, probably a distance of seven miles so he deserved 'A' for effort.

In 1977 as part of a motor sports event at Silverstone I was one of the film crew with all the advantages of behind the scenes freedom. I met up with a number of my road racing heros from the 1940s and 50s and from a tantalising list of stars, recorded interviews with Alan Jefferies, Maurice Cann, Freddy Frith, Jock West and Syd Barnett. Syd's mechanic for many years was Jim Baines and during a break for tea as we were discussing old motorcycles, he happened to mention that he had a 1937 BSA 250cc B22 Empire Star that was complete and he wanted it out of his shed. Perhaps it was now my turn to be hasty, for there and then I said I would have it with the intention of restoring it as a token replacement for the B18 model I had been weaned on.

It was a complete machine but had last been taxed in 1952 and the ensuing years standing in a shed had not been too kind to paintwork or chrome. It was going to be a challenge but at least I could offer it a brick shelter in which to undertake my first motorcycle restoration. At the time this was not going to be an easy task. I was contracted to ITN 'News at Ten' on what would be now termed as 24/7 call out. Even if the phone had not rung for two days, there was no guarantee that it would not ring on the third, perhaps just as you had your hands inside the gearbox!

As part of my initiation to motorcycle restoration, I was introduced to the world of auto jumbles at a time when an abundance of parts was available. Walter Green, a vintage Yorkshireman once referred to it as, "the harvest period" when you could virtually, go in with nothing and leave with most of a vintage machine. In later years in conversation with Titch Allen, he likened the first restoration to becoming a parent for the first time. It was what you wanted to do but you had no previous knowledge of how to do it. To pay homage to Titch would be superfluous for many far better scribes than I have already done it. Suffice to say, when I took over the Editorship from Jeff Clew of the Association of Pioneer Motorcyclists newsletter, Titch was a fountain of suggestions and guidance.

The nature of my work meant you could not plan days in advance, so it was a slow restoration compared to some whose work I have long admired in the motorcycling press. And yes, I made all the usual mistakes. Cellulose on top of gloss. Finishing the tank before checking it had no leaks and miscalculating the length of spokes. It would be close to six years before I could declare it finally ready for the road, but if I wanted to be pedantic, I would have to deduct the best part of twelve months for my work covering the Nationwide miners strike, when I saw a great deal more of hotel suites than my favourite arm chair.

But now I had good storage those six years had not been entirely barren. I was given a hedge find (as opposed to a barn find). This was a complete Royal Enfield 125cc, the 'Flying Flea' model and although I prepared and primered most of the metalwork, two strokes were never my forte and I passed this on to someone with more enthusiasm than myself. Then I had a telephone call from a work colleague. His brother-in-law was clearing a house in Leicester and in the cellar was a motorcycle which I could take away. Thinking it would be a wasted journey, probably finding the remains of some Japanese lightweight, I was pleasantly surprised to find most of a 1951 BSA B31 plunger model.

It was manufactured at the time when there was a shortage of nickel due to the Korean War. So there was little chrome ware to worry about. The hard part was how to get it out of the cellar. The situation became easier when the builder said as he intended making a basement flat he would knock out an entrance with easy access stairs and it was soon at street level. It turned into a beautifully restored machine. Not by me I hasten to add, but by a dear friend who was taken from us far too early, that Triumph supremo, Hughie Hancox. Hughie began his career at Coventry Motor Mart so knew his way around BSAs. I even had two offers from buyers before Hughie's work was completed. I rode the machine at a number of midland events over a three year period, then, as so often happens, I needed to raise money for a house move and it was a case of 'needs must when the devil drives'. Have I used that expression before?

But then another machine came into the stable. I had already met Jim Lee who was, and still is, Ariel Marque Specialist for the Vintage Motorcycle Club. Jim was a tester at Triumph and of course was a good friend of Hughie Hancox and he too was involved in a house move, with a need to 'farm' out some of his collection on a temporary loan basis. So

I now had use of an Ariel 350cc NG Deluxe on a simple arrangement whereby I taxed and insured it and carried out the usual maintenance work. I have fond memories of the Ariel and I used it on a number of VMCC Midland runs. One of them was the Bob Curry Run, with Bob in attendance, starting from the railway museum at Tyseley, Birmingham. Dad and Mum were down from Yorkshire and I have a treasured photo of him sitting on it with Mum in the background. It was possibly the last time he sat astride a motorcycle, nevertheless, he was keen to have a little potter around the car park and it was only the intervention of Mum with a mocking admonishment that deterred him.

When you are interested in old motorcycles there are two factors that fellow motorcyclists will concur with. You don't so much collect them, but acquire them. The other being having space available, you feel the need to fill it. With an expanding number of acquirements, there was one BSA model missing. My affection for the M20 in the mid fifties has already been recorded in earlier pages, so now seemed to be a favourable time to scan the pages of the motorcycle press.

There seemed to be an abundance of telescopic fork machines, both rigid and plunger available, but I had to advertise for a girder fork model. Eventually, I was offered a 1948 example, which in reality was a WD type that Small Heath merely changed the paint colour from Khaki to silver and black. But it provided me with all the familiar M20 traits I had come to love, especially that hill climbing ability that Dad had nicknamed 'BSA Slog', achieved by merely moving the ignition lever towards retard and letting the engine do the rest to the top of the climb.

Once again it became a familiar entry at Midland VMCC events, often in company with BSA aficionado, Gordon Jeal, who had an identical 1945 model. We would sometimes enter as a BSA M20 team and in paying respect to his seniority and expertise with everything BSA, I always addressed him as 'Skipper'. Gordon had first found his way around WD machines during his war service with the REME and while serving in North Africa he came to the conclusion that no matter what the conditions were, and these ranged from blistering heat to sand storms and constantly moving sand dunes it was the M20 that withstood the rigours and harsh treatment, including the cruelty inflicted by the despatch riders right boot, with the least problems.

Still showing my penchant for 250cc BSAs, I was offered a late 1946 C11 which, as indicated by the frame number, was one of the first to receive telescopic forks. Once again, this was to be a long drawn out restoration and even after 25 years, the speedometer has not yet reached 2000 miles.

It may be regarded as grey porridge in large dollops, but if you are looking to recapture those early post war years, when country lanes still featured horse drawn traffic, cycling clubs and an occasional car belonging to the local doctor or vet, then it has all the period charm to help you achieve it.

4:   1991 to 2016

Then I fell in love! All because of a classified advertisement in Old Bike Mart and we are still talking motorcycles I hasten to add. It was April, 1991 and my birthday was nearing and I just happened to be sitting beside the Settle to Carlisle railway line at Ais Gill summit. Why? I hear you chorus. I was waiting to record the sound of a recently restored steam locomotive, the 'Duchess of Hamilton'. Due to late running I had at least two hours to fill and I had spotted an advertisement for a BSA B25 fitted with the larger B40 engine. It was only down the road at Penrith so off I went.

As I walked into the garage at Stan Harper's house I had one of those feelings, no doubt similar to those that people on the road to Damascus experience. It was finished in Peony Red which was used on the B44 Victor. Within minutes a deal was done and 26 years and many miles later I would be very reluctant to part with it. Not only for the pleasure I have derived from the machine, but the friendship formed between VMCC Lakeland stalwart, Stan Harper and his wife, Grace. Over the years I have taken part in section runs organised by him and signed in at check points on Titch Allen's bi-annual Relay Rally that were manned by Stan and Grace. If anyone was looking to explain what the Vintage Motorcycle Club is about, then the foregoing lines will give some guidance.

I delayed collecting the B25 until my birthday, taking the train to Penrith with my riding gear. I had purposely planned to ride through the Yorkshire Dales, calling at Leeds to show Dad and Mum my new purchase. While Dad enthused about how modern it appeared to be, sadly Mum's health was rapidly deteriorating and she barely knew who I was. Within days I was back to make the necessary funeral arrangements.

I intend to move forward to 1993 fairly rapidly. It was that period in life that cannot be avoided nor can it be postponed or delayed. For almost sixty years my parents had nursed, cared, guided and supported me with little or no protest, until such a day comes when you have no parents. A void in any life that can only be faced by the individual. Being told to look to the future holds no certainty, only the past is real with it's timeless memories. For me, I have no complaints.

I needed some form of therapy to take away the grief and yet form a bond of retention and if there was a link to motorcycling it would serve as an added keepsake. The answer lay in a shaft drive BMW and through a colleague who was a member of the owners club, I had access to their magazine and classified advertisements. As I scanned the columns of R80s, R100s and even the new range of 1100 cc; there must have been a little deja vu pricking my conscience and telling me that you don't need all that power. Or as Dad would have put it, "why use four screws when two will do?"

It was the advertisement for a 1982 R65 that caught my eye and being a Nottingham address I was there the next day. Did I fall in love again? Probably. The seller was only the second owner and with only 26000 miles and the rare blue metallic finish, yet another deal was concluded. Once again my 'hoarding' nature indicates that all the right boxes must have been ticked, for as the ensuing years will reveal, it is still a no nonsense, reliable and comfortable machine to ride. Has everything to hold a place in modern day traffic and copes equally well with a 200 mile journey or a ride around the lanes over the Yorkshire Wolds as part of my local VMCC section events.

I met a man, as you do, at a midlands auto jumble. We were both looking for BSA parts and in the conversation he mentioned that he had most parts of a 1937 M20, the first year it was manufactured. The original engine had been discarded, as most were, having a design fault whereby the timing gears ran directly into bushes in the timing cover and not in the out-rigger plate of all subsequent engines. So it was an ex-army engine that came with it. He promised to send me a photograph, indicating all the parts and duly did. It was certainly all there and other than cables, a headlight and number plates, was certainly worth the price he was asking. It even had the original BSA brake and clutch levers, later stolen from the machine while it was parked at Drayton School,Banbury while attending the Banbury Run. It was Titch Allen who summed up the theft when I told him it was not what I expected from like-minded motorcyclists with, "In every barrel of apples, there has to be a rotten one."

The M20 had gone together with few problems and I wanted a machine that resembled those of the immediate post war period and not a 'toffee apple' example of later years. My memory from early teen years was not embellished with such words as, restored, classic or pristine. I like to describe it as, 'sympathetically restored'. There is a little story about this machine that may suggest a boding or perception beforehand of fate, which is not my intention. When I arrived home and unloaded the contents of the car, my then partner, Lois, stood in amazement and asked what I intended doing with all the parts. I told her I was going to put them together and ride it. In her usual playful way she answered, "Well I hope I live long enough to see you do it!" Six months later she died following a heart attack. The M20 now carries a discreet brass plaque with a simple dedication.

My working life was slowly petering away. Being a freelance technician in the world of film and television, I had been used to being told when to turn up for work. Now with my sixtieth birthday behind me and modern technology enabling companies to cut the number of crew members required, it was time to take stock and consider more leisure time rather than the workaholic lifestyle I had pursued. I now had an assorted collection of motorcycles and while there was nothing to become too excited over, I felt that they should be put to better use in mileage terms, rather than a country lane potter or a VMCC local section run.

Since being a schoolboy and having read the exploits of Ivan Hart-Davies and his heroic ride from John O'Groats to Land's End in 29 hours 12 minutes in 1911, I had quietly filed it away for one of those possible achievements in later years. In 1993, having held a motorcycle licence for over 40 years, I applied to join the Association of Pioneer Motorcyclists whose Newsletter was edited by Jeff Clew. Being an ardent speedway fan, he wrote asking if I would like to contribute some articles for publication, and in passing I mentioned an interest in completing an end to end run.

Jeff also had thoughts of raising money for a local charity by making the journey, so began our plans for 1993. I was going to be responsible for the route planning, while Jeff would take care of the accommodation and raising sponsorship. As the weeks went by, more people were asking to take part causing problems, not only with the administration, but with accommodation as the hotels and guest houses were asking for payment in advance. It was now turning into an ordeal rather than an occasion of a few dedicated motorcyclists fulfilling an ambition. So the idea foundered and I had to look elsewhere. Jeff was also busy compiling a book manuscript and was trying to meet his publisher's deadline. However, he still found time to take part in several events around Somerset and I accompanied him on a number of runs, such as the 'Five Valleys Run and the more prestigious sounding, 'Circuito Del Mendip', for which I won the furthest ridden award.

Early in 1994 an advertisement appeared in the VMCC Journal inviting interested members to take part in an end to end run, starting from John O'Groats. The suggestion being that entrants would sponsor themselves in aid of raising money for the British Heart Foundation. The man behind the project was Bob Fisher, a leading light in the Swindon Section and later to become a modest impresario when it came to organising motorcycle tours throughout the British Isles. To take part in an end to end run you have to consider the logistics involved, for no matter what part of the country you live in, somehow you have to get to your start point and even if you live in Cornwall, you are in effect doing the run twice. I made several enquiries with haulage companies and found none of them interested. Then in my innocence I approached British Railways. Had I not put my speedway machine on a train in Leeds bound for King's Cross back in 1958. I still have a vivid recollection of the look of shock horror on the face of the railway official at my request. When I gave him my 1958 example it was dismissed with a churlish answer about being before he was born.

The problem was resolved by Bob Fisher when he realised that with a growing entry now over sixty, and many of them asking if there were facilities for transporting machines, it was becoming obvious that transport had to be hired, along with a deluxe coach to convey entrants to the start. My choice of machine was the BSA B25/B40, which in effect had now blossomed into a B44 with a change of engine to the redoubtable 441cc unit. The distance situation was now eased as all that was required of riders was to present their machines at Wooton Bassett and then join the coach for the long journey north, 14 hours in fact! The event had been planned in six stages, with overnight stops at Inverness, Helensburgh, Windermere, Buxton and Cheddar. Plus of course the hotels at Groats and Land's End.

Not wishing to drag out the narrative with too much repetition, we were after all only riding motorcycles through Scotland and England, I will sum up the whole week as one of the most pleasurable and satisfying of my entire motorcycling pursuit. Bob Fisher had planned the whole enterprise like a military operation. Our luggage was conveyed by van to each hotel, to be in the foyer as we arrived each day. Overnight secure parking in Kwik-Fit depots was available, they being one of the major sponsors. A daily back-up vehicle followed the route after the last rider had left each day and the camaraderie throughout was scintillating. Many of the allegiances formed were to continue with later tours, such as those to Ireland, repeat end to end tours and across the Channel in Europe.

It certainly spurred me to do something a little bit different, such as visiting the most northerly part of the British Isles, but in order to keep a sensible continuity,that is for later pages. 1995 was to become a fairly barren year in motorcycling for the reasons I have already indicated in an earlier paragraph. Bereavement is something no one can avoid and yet I suppose we all cope with it in different ways. Other than routine maintenance to retain a standard for the annual MOT test, my mileage fell to just over 400, whereas the previous years total had been over 5000. I was down but not out, if that makes any literary sense. To fill the days I began taking stock of the shelves of spares I had acquired and it became clear that I still had many parts for a JAP speedway engine. How many times have we told ourselves, 'I won't need these anymore.'

The usual classified 'Ad' was placed in Old Bike Mart and one of the first callers was a former rider, who although I was aware of his name, had never actually met in combat. Ian Paskin was to introduce me to vintage speedway racing, now becoming a popular second half attraction at various tracks throughout Britain. However, before I had been well and truly hooked, he had purchased a large quantity of my stock of spares.

Coventry Speedway was only 12 miles from my home and Ian had mentioned a forthcoming meeting that was to feature riders and machines of an earlier period. My period in fact. To see and hear machines from the 1950s with an open exhaust note, riders in black leathers with no hint of sponsorship names and that inevitable smell of burnt Methanol and Castrol R was all it took for me to consider a return to the track. Racing was staged to put on a show for the crowd and if you could also throw in an odd broadside or two around the bends, that was all it took to show the crowds how things used to be. There were no contracts to sign, nor promoters to put pressure on you if you were failing to produce a useful points tally and your original racing licence could be renewed. All I needed was a suitable machine.

Feelers were put out to see what might be available and some of the offers had to be rejected on sight due to very basic faults that certainly would not have been passed by the machine examiner. I received a call from someone in the north of England who had a complete machine that had a local pedigree, in so far as it had taken part in a demonstration ride at a northern speedway stadium. A further plus in it's favour when I arrived to look it over, was it started by the accepted method of spinning the back wheel. This was a good indication that at least the magneto functioned normally as did the dual feed Pilgim pump that was delivering oil soon after starting. A price was agreed and cash changed hands and within half an hour I was returning south with a speedway machine. Was it deja vu, summer madness, or a combination of both with a little bit of egotistic mid-life crisis in the mix for good measure.

Things began to move quickly. The JAP 500cc Speedway engine is of simple design and yet it packed a punch that gave it a brake horsepower output of 55BHP at 5500RPM, which at the peak of it's development, made it the most powerful single cylinder unsupercharged engine in the world. Despite this, it was a very simple engine to take apart and work on, which I did within 2 hours of unloading from the trailer. It was evident that it had not seen action in a racing sense for some time and although it was not being prepared for any, I replaced the valves, springs and piston rings, along with a partial nut and bolt restoration and it was ready for the first meeting.

This was to be at Peterborough as part of the BMF Annual show where vintage speedway was one of several activities around the racing circuit in front of a packed grandstand. My return to speedway after a lay off of 36 years could go two ways. Either I fall flat on my face in front of an expectant crowd or I could just follow the opposition around the track. I was in good company for on one side was a 1928 Douglas 'Dirt Track' model, to my right was a 1932 Rudge and on the outside a conventional JAP powered machine similar to mine. The announcer had already made it clear that this was my first appearance on a speedway track since 1960 and he had embroided some facts and figures to work the crowd into a state of fanatical coolness. Then came the moment of truth waiting for the tapes to go up. That feeling of commitment of you against the others, holding the throttle open just under peak revs so as to avoid bringing the front wheel up in the air, and keeping the clutch lever almost engaging to save mere milliseconds as you release it and feel the surge of power driving you forward as the steering gets lighter having little effect due to the front wheel not being in contact with the track for the first few yards.

Then you are confronted by a left hand bend and as you lay the machine over to the left the natural reaction is for the front wheel to begin sliding out of control drifting the machine out towards the fence. This is the critical moment, that moment of truth that equates to what I had heard the Spanish bullfighter describe as he went in for the kill. To combat this the throttle has to be opened to an almost flat out position to start the rear wheel sliding outwards, bringing the handlebars to a right lock position and regaining control of the front wheel. At this stage throttle control is all important. Once in a driving slide, the rider is able to place the front wheel where he wants to steer if he sees a gap opening. The real secret is determining how much wheel spin must be deployed to keep the rear wheel spinning and yet provide enough traction to drive both wheels forward, hopefully staying with the opposition.

I had presumed that the announcer's eulogy had aroused some curiosity amongst the crowd so my performance had better be good. From memory I recall thinking no matter what, don't stall the engine on the starting line. The tapes went up, the steering went light, the first bend came up and I found myself leading the pack. The Douglas and the Rudge soon fell behind, but the other rider matched me in straight line speed, if not around the bends. I sensed that I was probably under geared by one tooth but managed to hang on and crossed the line to receive the chequered flag. Vintage speedway racing was for me.

I returned to the pits with a wide grin, knowing that my performance had been watched by many of the other veterans who were ready with such plaudits as, "You can still do it." "Great stuff." Or, with a tinge of sarcasm, "You've got a promising career behind you." If I was walking tall that day, I was soon cut down to size a week later when booked to appear in the second half at Coventry. There is no place for dreaming in speedway as I was soon to learn. The reality was, I came from a previous age which was clearly evident as I followed the home team from the dressing room to the pits. All the young riders were bedecked in gaudy coloured leathers covered with company names of sponsors and as they passed the fans enclosure there were the constant requests for autographs and photographs, all accompanied by names such as, Wayne, Dean, Shane and Gary. As I passed by in sombre black leathers there wasn't a murmur.

It was another fun event and I was meeting up with more riders from my era, which was nice from a nostalgia angle, but depressing when faced with remarks such as, "I didn't know you were still around!" Coventry were in the National League but during my time at Southampton I had never ridden the track before. There was a reminder of the higher standard expected from first division riders when you walked out of the dressing room. Above the door a notice read, 'Winning isn't everything, it's the only thing.' A number of the tracks where we appeared did not exist in the 1960s and one booking meant a trip over the water, as far as Ryde on the Isle of Wight! The speedway press were kind to our dithering riding and performances and someone came up with the billing of 'The men in Black' which is still in use. However, supporters memories for speedway machines fitted with JAP engines is diminishing and the ever present hand of environmental regulations over silencing is taking away much of the period spectacle.

I was still notching up the miles using the BMW and the B44, now styled as a Victor 'Shooting Star' and since becoming involved with the Association of Pioneer Motorcyclists, there were regular trips to committee meetings held at Ripley, in Surrey. The BMW was used to accompany an old veteran motorcyclist to see a pal who lived near Cork in Southern Ireland. At the time, old Arthur was 76 and now restricted to riding a 125cc Honda, so it was a laborious journey to Holyhead and down through the Wicklow Mountains. I have long held a desire to return to Southern Ireland, taking in the west coast area, including the Ring of Kerry but to date it is still, to use that Americanism, on the back burner, although at 82 I still have ambitions.

One notable event I attended twenty years ago as I was returning from Brighton, having taken part in the Coventry to Brighton annual Run, was the 50th Anniversary of the founding of the Vintage Motor Motorcycle Club at the Lounge Cafe on the Hog's Back, Surrey. It was the 28th of April, 1996, exactly 50years later and at the same time that 105 members on motorcycles gathered in the presence of Titch Allen and founder member, Ken Garrard to celebrate the 'golden' day. Most people were of the opinion that, as they were unable to be at the inaugural gathering, this was the alternative as nobody would be around for the centenary celebrations. I took a lovely picture of Titch Allen being presented with a plaque by the Deputy Mayor of Guildford and, understandingly, he was very moved by the whole ceremony.

There were other memorable trips in 1996, one of which was to America. At the beginning of the year I had driven from Baltimore to Ohio to deliver a Volkswagen Beetle which had belonged to Lois. This was part of a bequest to a lady friend whom she had worked with during a three year stay in the sixties. I was invited back for a longer holiday during the summer months and was able to borrow a small sized Honda, enabling me to explore the vast region of the Amish community. These delightful people do not believe in mechanical transport, relying on the horse and buggy for daily use. The country lanes went on and on, although some of the surfaces were not to British County Council standards. Nevertheless, it was a wonderful experience on traffic free roads, and I mean traffic free. Just an occasional pony and trap. The only problem was avoiding the droppings, a drawback that our pioneer forefathers must have experienced too.

Before the speedway season ended in October, the 'Men in Black' were invited to several final meetings to stage one of our nostalgia pageants. The promoters thought it was a more fitting end to the season than a firework display. And probably cheaper. We were, however, warned that before we could appear in 1997, all vintage machines must be fitted with a suitable silencer. Environmental 'Elf! and Safety' was really taking over. With the dawn of 1997 came the surge in all things 'millennium'. Readers may recall the dire warnings that your microwave was going to cease working, computers would need re-programming and telephone number memories would be wiped out. I'm sure a great deal of money was made by inventive characters with elaborate looking test equipment, giving rides to those who always seem to be willing to be taken for one.

But motorcyclists are made of sterner stuff and not easily taken in. I hope! My mileage fell dramatically in 1997, due mainly to the weather. The Meteorological Office declared that June had been the wettest since records began and many motorcyclists could vouch for the accuracy of the statement. I missed a good number of section runs due to the weather, having an aversion against starting out in the rain. Oddly, if I am already into a journey there is not the same reluctance, knowing the Barbour suit, plus white towel around the neck in the style of Hugh Viney and many other top trials men, would virtually ensure a dry ride. At the start of 1998 as millennium mania grew, I made my only offering to marking the end of the old century by declaring I would ride a motorcycle on the very last day of December, 1999.

Yes I know it wasn't strictly the end of the century, but the changing year date was the thing most people were waiting for. Before that I was still logging good mileages mainly on the BMW and the B44. As for vintage speedway, I have to confess it was becoming something of an anti-climax. I knew there was nothing at the end of all the hype and acknowledging the crowds, so I made my last appearance towards the end of 1998. Fittingly, it was at Poole where I had ridden 38 years earlier and even more appropriate, it was between a team of Southampton veterans versus Poole, led by Bill Holden who had ridden for them in 1952!

My career in film and television also came to an end when I disposed of my equipment. This was quickly followed by the two speedway machines I had amassed for another plan was now formulating. I had been having some epic rides on the B44, taking in a large part of the Yorkshire Dales, including many of the roads covered back in 1948 on the pillion of the OK Supreme. As the recognised age of retirement beckoned, I began to yearn for my native roots of Yorkshire as the place to spend those, 'advancing years', as the life insurance brokers like to portray the period. I suppose it does have a kinder ring about it than being told, "You're getting old mate."

The obvious place to return was to Leeds, so in the spring of 1999 tentative enquiries were made with a number of estate agents. Houses had never made an impression on me, therefore my knowledge of buying and selling extended to no more than two in 65 years. It didn't have to be extravagant or have large gardens nor vast rooms for guests. All I stipulated was a modest sized workshop or useful out buildings, plus of course a limited price range. My lack of interest in the property market had left a huge gap in my understanding of the economics and high finance of the property ladder, to say nothing of inflation. A simple example of prices passing me by is evident in the sale of Dad's house, which went on the market in 1993 for £47,000. By 2003 it was being offered at £135,000 and in 2013 at £205,000. I wonder where I went wrong?

What became perfectly clear was any thoughts of a return to the City of my birth were not realistic. The only solution was to turn eastwards having been given some guidance as to prices in an area radiating from Selby, between the rivers Aire and Ouse. I knew the district reasonable well, having had motorcycling pals here in the fifties. In fact by one of those strange twists of fate, the village where I now live actually had two petrol stations which I remember patronising and often stopped for half a gallon! The local paper was published every Thursday and I was usually in the printing office early to collect a copy hot off the press. A picture 'AD' for a modest bungalow caught my eye, not only for a neat kept appearance but it clearly showed a double garage at the end of the drive. Within an hour I had done an external viewing, called at the estate agents to register my interest and arranged for a survey to be carried out. And the rest, as they say, is history.

Wheels were put into motion in the midlands, which of course like many house sales, did not run smooth. It seemed nothing was going to happen before the end of the year so my date with destiny was still on. Or to put it another way, riding a motorcycle on the final day of the last month of the twentieth century, which I achieved, just. I had chosen the BSA B44 for reasons of sentiment, but found the battery was low and insufficient to power the electronic ignition. Even worse, I had loaned my Optimate trickle battery charger to a colleague. It was a dismal day with a hint of drizzle so there was a necessity for running lights to add to the problem. The only solution was to remove the battery from my car and connect flying leads to the BSA battery.

The engine started and to try and ease the situation, I screwed the throttle stop to give a fast tick over while I put on my riding gear. Later than planned, I was off along the country lanes of Leicestershire with the ammeter showing a healthy charge. Care had to be taken as the lanes were treacherous with damp leaves everywhere and care was needed in applying the brakes. This was proved a few minutes later when I rounded a bend and was confronted by a young girl exercising her pony. A sharp rear brake application locked the wheel and before I could catch the throttle, the engine had stalled. The young girl smiled sweetly, thinking I had stopped the engine to avoid startling her mount. My thoughts were, if the engine doesn't restart, I am in trouble, last day of the century or not. Fortune must have favoured the brave for with one prod on the kickstart, that old thumper was running as well as ever. Tomorrow we were starting with the calendar showing 2000, but for now I was still in the old century and enjoying that glorious feeling of man's basic conception of an internal combustion engine propelling me along. It was one of the most enjoyable 60 miles of my life.

The first day of the new century began like any other. The microwaves all over the country still worked, as did computer programmes and telephone systems. I likened all the prophets of doom to those who predict the world ending by a certain date. I have often wondered how they explain it when the date passes and we are all still here. Before I could begin to think about motorcycles in the new century there was the matter of a house move to Yorkshire to complete, which, fortunately, was progressing smoothly. I had to make separate arrangements for transporting the motorcycles as the removal company were not prepared to include them in with the rest of the chattels, so the collection arrived some days after the furniture.

Being situated at the lower fringe of the Vale of York, around 10 metres above sea level in fact, may have been the reason why February was a mild month. Nevertheless, it was an ideal opportunity to sample the local lanes, many of which were familiar from earlier years. But it was not an auspicious start, for the BSA B44 was still presenting battery problems by not holding charge. By good fortune, the village where I had chosen to settle was also home to two long standing VMCC members with a wealth of knowledge in all things connected with old motorcycles and how to keep them running, so it was to them I turned for help in locating all the usual suppliers of spare parts, both new and used. I was also introduced to the man who had welding equipment, lathes, milling machines and all those tools that are normally beyond the pocket of the average motorcyclist. I am convinced that there is such a man in most towns that over the years have kept thousands of motorcyclists on the road and long may they continue.

It was several weeks before I became accustomed to the routine of following a route over the Yorkshire Wolds, without the thought of a long journey home and passing through two other counties before arriving. Being back in my native county was already a good feeling and I was already planning some extended trips. One of Titch Allens's many legacies so far as the Vintage Motorcycle Club was concerned, was his brilliant idea of a Relay Rally on a bi-annual basis. To the non member not familiar with it's staging, this is a simple non-competitive event which takes in over fifty check points around Britain, manned by members providing refreshments and usually near to petrol stations. The idea is to try and visit as many check points as you wish, each one providing a sticker for your route card and you can ride alone or with fellow club members at whatever speed you choose.

Entry forms arrived via the monthly Journal and I was soon plotting a route starting from my local section in East Yorkshire. Then I headed south to Bilsthorpe in Nottinghamshire, continuing to Quorn in Leicestershire where my previous local section, The Taverners, had set up their checkpoint at the Great Central Railway station. From there I linked up with other members who were heading for the Club's Headquarters at Burton upon Trent, a visit which has proved to be my only attendance at 'HQ' since joining in 1980. Then it was on to Leek in Staffordshire with a couple of local members from that section. By this time my intake of cups of tea was double the number of checkpoints I had signed in at and I was at the furthest point from my home base. The remainder of the journey was probably the most scenic, taking in the high points of Derbyshire and South Yorkshire, including the climb over Holme Moss, followed by the delightful descent into 'Last of the Summer Wine' country.

For the remainder of the journey I was amongst heavy traffic as Sunday shoppers were heading for home too. There was also the West Riding road surfaces to contend with, a long standing bone of contention with Yorkshire Motorcyclists. The final result was I had visited five checkpoints and logged 276 miles, a target I have not bettered since.

After I had completed the end to end run way back in 1994, I was left with a nagging feeling of doing something that was a little bit different and yet feasible, something that few people would have completed and yet giving that feeling of satisfaction, to say nothing of an enjoyable holiday. I began to look at the possibility of taking a motorcycle to the most northerly point of the British Isles, at least so far as public roads were concerned and this would mean visiting the most northerly Island of the Shetland group, the Isle of Unst. Study of the map showed that the road terminated at a point known as Skaw Bay so this became my target.

By chance I saw a feature on UK Motorcycle clubs in Classic Motorcycle magazine and found a Shetland Motorcycle Club listed, including the name and address of the secretary. My original intention was just to try and obtain information of accommodation and the possibility of reaching Skaw Bay with a motorcycle, however, my initial enquiry prompted a very friendly and lengthy reply from Secretary, Joe Gray, who just happened to have recently retired from a position with Shetland Islands Council Road Maintenance Department. Furthermore, he indicated that not only could he recommend guest house accommodation, he was willing to accompany me on tours around the Islands, culminating in a final day trip to Skaw Bay. It proved to be just another example of the camaraderie that makes the motorcycle fraternity a little bit special. On the day of my departure, he accompanied me to the ferry terminal in Lerwick on his Rudge Ulster.

Joe not only had an intimate knowledge of all the roads throughout the Islands, he was known by so many people we came into contact with. These could be Curators at museums, shopkeepers, even the ferryboat skippers as we crossed from the Mainland to Yell, or from Yell to Unst. This meant we were always invited to travel on the bridge during each crossing, which on one occasion allowed me the opportunity to have control of the boat. Alright, I know I only had my hand on the wheel, but it's a good conversation opener if I ever need to use it. I suppose some would ask why I wanted to make the trip to Skaw Bay. My answer would be the same as a mountaineer gives when asked why he climbed Everest. Because it's there! Fortunately, it had not been commercialised, at least not in 2001. There were no candy floss stalls or bingo halls, just pure tranquillity. Plus the thought of knowing you are further north than Stockholm or Leningrad. (St. Petersburg). A beach pebble now adorns my hearth.

For this trip I had chosen the BMW R65 because of the better luggage facilities provided by the standard BMW panniers. To be able to remove them in seconds and walk into your accommodation does make life easier. My total trip miles added up to 1208 with an average MPG of 58 and the only problem encountered was one of the pannier frames fracturing. I was guided to a local farmer who had an arc welder and before commencing the repair, he warned that because of the chrome finish, he could only make a temporary 'get you home' job. I have always intended to make a more permanent repair but I have to confess, 15 years later it is still holding!

Now I had more space my next decision was to purchase a bench lift to make life easier. Kneeling alongside a motorcycle is fine when you are under 40 and still have healthy knee joints, but as the French say, "Tempus Fugit!" So why not make things easy on yourself. Once more I met a man, on this occasion at a VMCC rally, who told me he had some BSA M20 parts to dispose of and for a modest sum I could take them away. It was that old story where you walk into a man's workshop to purchase some spare parts and under a sheet in the corner there is the outline of an old motorcycle. This turned out to be a 1954 BSA C10L in running order and although the registration number had been sold, it had been given an 'A' plate. Already I can sense readers muttering words such as, an obsession with grey porridge, or get a life! But as more learned people than I have said, "In retirement, the secret is to stay active."

The C10L was an easy restoration and an ideal machine for taking to local rallies for static display, if only to count the number of people who would come up and say, "I had one of those." In the meantime, the mileage was mounting on the M20 with section rallies and most trips were well over 100 miles. To reach section starting points was usually a round trip of 70 or more miles, so three figure mileages were not uncommon and were always accomplished with the usual M20 aplomb, to which I am sure many old despatch riders would nod knowingly.

The B44 Victor was taken off the road during 2001 for a major overhaul. Engine wise, it was still performing well but the transmission was now in need of attention with replacement of all sprockets and chains, along with clutch plates and centre bearing. As there was no urgency to complete the work and having the M20 available for most section runs, it was 2002 before it was ready for a test run, appropriately on my birthday in April. However, with a lapse of Sunday events during the high summer of 2001, I attended a true vintage pre 1931 meeting and found a whole new world of motorcycling opening up. This was organised by a small club dedicated to the use of older machines and was in fact a breakaway from the main Vintage Motorcycle Club and known as the Yorkshire Vintage Motorcyclists. It was another of those road to Damascus occasions where I found myself seeing the charm and basic simplicity of earlier motorcycles.

I began recalling that for many years past, my old work colleague, Les Brumpton, had often asked me when we were discussing motorcycle manufacturers, if I had ever heard of a York. His interest only stemmed from his younger days at a nearby farm in Lincolnshire where he often saw it under sheets of corrugated metal. As the name meant nothing to me either, it was usually dismissed with no further thought. That is until one day, having been given a copy of Erwin Tragatsch's classic, 'Illustrated Encyclopedia of Motorcycles' and finding not only an entry under York, but an accompanying illustration from a catalogue.

Les and I were still in contact even though we were both officially retired and I would sometimes call to see him on my way to a BMW spares supplier at Surfleet in Lincolnshire. It was on such a trip that I mentioned the old motorcycle still languishing in the barn, but now with several more layers of lumber added. The old farmer had since died and the farm had been passed on to his two sons who both knew the history of the derelict motorcycle. Their father had served in the army and towards the end of the war had been in Austria during the time it was under the control of Allied armies. It seems he had commandeered the York for daily use and when the time came for their unit to be returned to England, he considered it to be part of his war reparation and loaded the machine as part of a returning convoy. This is believed to have been in 1946 and it would appear that it was never used on English roads as it never received a registration number. The eldest son did have a vague recollection of riding on the pillion of an old motorcycle as a child, but was unable to confirm it being the York.

The brief entry in Tragatsch gave me enough information to start researching the name at the Coventry Museum of Transport archives, although detailed information was lacking, other than the address of the factory, which had been where the Omega motorcycle was built until the company failed in 1927. The Works Manager, William Green, had taken over the factory and began producing a very basic British style of motorcycle to a design by an Austrian entrepreneur named Robert Sturm. By describing it as a basic British style of the period, indicates that most components were bought in. The engine was a 500cc JAP s.v. The gearbox was Sturmey Archer, while the forks were the early pattern by Webb. The only part made in house was probably the frame, which bears a close resemblance to an Ariel of that period. Hardly surprising, because my research found that William Green had been making frames for Ariel and other manufacturers, probably to keep his workforce employed during this difficult period.

My research in this country found little about Robert Sturm and it was only when I made contact with other owners in Austria that his background became known. Although it may have lost something in the translation, it seems his business methods were open to question, a 'Jack the Lad' for want of a better term. There was no doubt he had a flair for impact advertising which was pure fantasy. He dealt only in cash, taking the customers payment before the machine had been built, or certainly before it arrived in Austria and when his agreement with William Green ended in 1930, it was due to Sturm moving over the border into Germany to avoid unpaid taxes. Yet he continued to assemble motorcycles, now using other power units such as Sturmey Archer. To date, including mine, there are 9 York motorcycles surviving. There is also most of another but without an engine. And why the name York? Nothing is forthcoming in Austria as to the origin and we can only surmise that Robert Sturm with his flair for salesmanship, thought a good solid sounding English name would help his sales campaign.

In delivering the potted history of the York, once more I have to crave your indulgence for allowing my narrative to leap ahead, so may I remind you how we began discussing the marque. I had arrived at the farm near Boston in Lincolnshire with my old work colleague, Les Brumpton. Les had in fact alerted the two brothers of my interest and a start had been made to clear the barn. Despite this, it still took close to an hour before most of the machine was visible. They say first impressions count most, although to be truthful, mine were slowly ebbing as each piece of timber, old carpet and sacking was removed. It soon became clear that over the years, close to sixty in fact, if anyone wanted a nut or bolt or piece of metal bracket, the York had become a DIY donor. I was also becoming concerned that the brothers were convincing themselves that there was a pot of gold at the end of the rubbish pile, borne out by one of them constantly wiping a rag over parts as they slowly emerged into daylight again.

When the time came to try and wheel it into the daylight I really was convincing myself that I should settle for riding the M20 in VMCC events if I was looking for a feeling of nostalgia. Both tyres had been in contact with the ground and this was just an earth floor, while the wheel rims were giving a good impression of Nottingham lace and the front just folded at the first attempt of any forward movement. It may have worked in my favour, for one of the brothers came out with, "It looks like you've not a lot left to start with." As it was delivered in that delightful Lincolnshire accent, I was forced to smile at his choice of words. But when he added, "I reckon it ain't worth a lot." I began to feel that I had the bare bones of a vintage project, even more so when he accepted my offer.

I returned a week later with a trailer and a large blue plastic sheet to hide the rusty remains as I drove up through Lincolnshire, still with a feeling of apprehension. Any thoughts of breasting Sun Rising Hill one day were quickly dismissed. Once again my plan was to sympathetically restore it to fit in with my memories of machines in the very early post war years when the brightest part was the rear chain! I also allowed myself a tinge of regret that Dad would not hear it running. Having a rare name would have intrigued him, as he would often recall long forgotten makers from the boom period of the early twenties. By the time it was unloaded onto my garage floor, the remains looked an impossible task so far as restoration was concerned. It had all the appearance of a machine that had been put together very cheaply, although the price shown in Robert Sturm's 1929 catalogue was 2000 Austrian Shillings.

Trying to turn the engine over produced an ominous sound of a conrod moving in the cylinder and unconnected to the piston. Which is exactly what I found when lifting the barrel. At some time the piston had been removed and there was evidence of a seizure having occurred and a rebore would be required at some future date. The magneto was missing, but suprisingly, the Pilgrim pump was intact. Which was a relief for if there was one component on a vintage engine which suffers from inexperienced hands tampering, it is the external oil pump. Further investigation revealed a sound big end, at least there was no movement, but the main bearings had suffered from half a century of water entry to the crankcase, aided by a missing spark plug.

The Sturmey Archer gearbox was in better internal condition, due to the liberal quantity of grease,although again, years of standing had turned this into an almost solid compound of yellow fat which no longer served to lubricate the gears. As for the rest, the frame and forks were remarkably free from corrosion. The wheel hubs looked to be sound and the petrol tank had evidence of oil having been put in at some time. So all was not doom and gloom, although I was not setting myself any targets or deadlines. I was also sidetracked for a while when someone offered me a 600cc sv JAP engine as an alternative and in my innocence, I started to try and fit this. So started a long learning curve about JAP industrial engines. It became my John Logie Baird moment. The right medium but pursuing a false path to a dead end.

In the 1930s when more manufacturers began to produce their own engines, the resultant falling sales at J.A.Prestwich was counteracted by them developing a range of industrial engines based around their tried and tested designs of motorcycle engines. The range of products is too numerous to detail here, but a brief guide lists, generator sets, Lister trucks for factory use (the forerunner of the Fork Lift Truck) and narrow gauge locomotives used in clay pits and brick works. All of these variations had a common factor. They were designed to run at a constant speed. This meant port openings were limited and cam wheel profiles were more gentle. Without this knowledge I wasted a great deal of time (and money) trying to adapt the engine for everyday road performance. I recall one test out on the Yorkshire Wolds on a long straight gradient, while making the climb in second gear, I was overtaken by two cyclists on machines that probably had eight times the gears I had available.

This seemingly grand obsession with restoring the York had not taken over my activities entirely, although the initial impetus for pre 1931 motorcycling was becoming a little faded. I was still involved in section runs and because of my geographical location, I had a choice of events. Throughout 2003 and 2004 I added nearly 5000 miles to the B44 and M20. As for the BSA 250cc 'C' models, these were mainly involved in static shows or short country lane jaunts. My inherited habit of logging machine mileages persists to this day and I now seem to have settled on an annual target of 6000 per annum. Not always achieved, admittedly, which I put down to indifferent summers and a high mileage body!

On one occasion in 2004 I strayed further afield to take part in a Lakeland Section run on the B44 notching up 280 miles in the process. It was also a reunion meeting with Stan and Grace Harper, who were pleased to see the old red 'Beeza' again. The R65 was also involved in high mileage trips, two of them to Old Warden for vintage aeroplane events which of course was another of my leisure pursuits. It was while returning from one of these visits that the R65 failed for the second time with an electrical fault. Eight years earlier it had been an ignition coil failure. This time it was the trigger unit for the electronic ignition.

It was now time to become serious and make an all out effort to get the York running by finding a piston for the original engine. Despite covering auto jumbles from Garstang to Newark and Scorton to Cheltenham, another six months drifted by and another year passed into 2007. The difficulty was the unusual size of bore which was 88.7mm, then I had to consider how much would need to be taken out to remove scoring in the cylinder which was compounded by the fact it was a fixed cylinder head and probably difficult to mount on the standard boring bar. Scorton auto jumble, near Catterick in North Yorkshire was the third Saturday in each month, however, being January, I was reluctant to attend. Not only for the fact it was too soon after the festivities, but the weather did not encourage early rising. You are probably pre-empting what I am leading up to for I made the effort and went, arriving just in time to find a vendor unloading his van, which included a tray of various boxed pistons and yes, there was a yellow Hepolite box clearly marked 88.7mm plus 40 thou. Oversize. It was like finding the Holy Grail!

The first thing I did upon arriving home was download an entry form for the Banbury Run and following completion, drove to York to ensure it was collected the same day. As Del Boy Trotter always said, "He who dares, wins." Realistically, I had five months to complete the engine and ensure all cycle parts were functioning to MOT standards. The man who could do all things was contacted and gave an assurance that, not only could he handle the reboring, he would ensure that the piston did not foul the flywheels. A week or so later, I received from the DVLA, my age related number, appropriately with two letters and four digits. To achieve this I had to take the machine, by trailer, into their office in Leeds fitted with the industrial engine and of course I was apprehensive over the fact of an engine number that did not tally with what I had declared. Being a rainy day I had fitted a full cover to keep out road spray and began to remove this for when the inspecting officer arrived.

A smartly dressed young man who must have been at least 22, took one look under the sheet, saw there was a motorcycle there, made two ticks on his sheet and with a wave was gone. I'm sure it must be harder now. But for the first time since arriving in England, the York had a registration number. The Sturmey Archer gearbox needed a modification to replace that strange design of a double-sided cup and cone bearing. As I later came into contact with other vintage riders using a similar type of gearbox, it seemed to be a recommended alteration to ensure trouble free running. One problem which caused a delay as I ticked off the calendar days to June 17 were the steering head bearings. They were not a perfect fit in the frame, although the dimensions appeared to be an Imperial size. I thought it very unlikely these would have been replaced during the years in Austria, and yet there was no size listed in the usual bearing stockists I contacted that would have been a perfect fit. I began to worry with each turn of the calendar page.

Once again, there was a man who had a lathe and suggested a modification using readily available taper roller bearings, he even made a small end bush to complete the engine work and to this day, both are serving their purpose well. It shows what a wonderful cottage industry we have around our Islands with hidden skills in all types of obscure locations. I hope people who live in thatched cottages are able to find such talents to help with their preservation needs.

As Banbury neared, I realised my technique with a hand change machine was inadequate in heavy traffic, it now being 30 years since I had been riding the 1936 250cc BSA on a regular basis. Another factor which many motorcyclists will be familiar with, is during that 30 year lapse cars had become much faster and were driven accordingly by drivers who had no experience of road craft on two wheels. I did, therefore, feel somewhat vulnerable in a slow moving stream of traffic with the problem of a 3-speed gearbox, where second gear is too high and first too low. Young impatient drivers with an attitude of, 'I didn't get where I am today by crawling behind some old crock,' were no help either. Only by ignoring some of the verbal abuse such as, "You're going the wrong way for Brighton," or, "Why don't you scrap it and buy a push bike," did I become determined to fly the flag for vintage motorcycling.

In June, 2007 yet another ambition was achieved as I lined up at the start of the Banbury Run, from Drayton School, Banbury. I had entered for the Class C Timed category and was hoping to average 24 MPH to qualify for any award. But a prize was not the object, it was the challenge of making it up Sun Rising Hill without floundering to a halt at the first bend in front of the usual audience that gathers every year. In fact this was the first year that marshals were not allowed on the hill due to a recently introduced Insurance ruling. Old vintage men had told me that the secret is to select the correct gear in good time before the bend and retain this to the top. Trying to change gear on the steepest part of the climb where the side banking is close to the road, is the worst place to falter.

Things started well. I had a clear run as the climb began and was into second gear well before the bend. I was now becoming used to the vagaries of the Binks 2-jet carburettor and made a subtle adjustment to the air control to which the engine began to respond, aided by me nudging the ignition lever towards retard. This was sufficient for the engine to settle into a pulling mode as the gradient steepened. Earlier in the climb, I had noted a small car up ahead but assumed that this would have cleared the hill before I arrived. I was wrong. I suddenly realised I was closing fast on a Ford Fiesta being driven by an elderly lady who appeared to be in difficulties in selecting a lower gear and was showing signs of stalling. My only real option was to try and overtake providing there was no descending traffic and as it was becoming clear the Ford was labouring in the wrong gear, I went for a change into first gear. For what ever reason, the lever jumped out of gear just as I was overtaking the now distressed lady and I had to use my left hand to hold the control in the first notch, while holding the throttle wide open.

To the onlooker it must have been a bizarre scene as I came over the crest of the hill, partly on the wrong side of the road and with both hands over to the offside of the machine. Should there be any photographic evidence of my first Banbury at this point on the course, my number was 383 and I can be contacted through the publisher. Even though I was now only 4 miles from the finishing line I had told myself, as my old head master often did, "Can do better!" And I did, but we have to wait until 2010. My verdict on the day as I drove back to Yorkshire was one of elation, satisfaction and gratification. I had put the engine together with all the skills passed on to me by Dad and I mused about the time I had watched him split the crankcase on the OK Supreme and drive out the worn bush, then after fitting the new part, we went off on a motorcycling holiday That had been a JAP engine too. It helped me to appreciate what motorcycling was all about in those early years of the 20th Century, when a rider merely accepted that any mechanical contrivance, however simple must have lapses that you learned to cope with, just as you do when life throws one of those unexpected moments of grief into an otherwise simple lifestyle. Without wishing to sound too reverent, riding a motorcycle is just another art form.

Flushed with success, or at least the reliability of the York and my appreciation of old motorcycles, I entered for the Northern Veteran Run. This was, and still is, a Mid Lincs. Section of a VMCC event, organised by Stuart Parker, from whom I had purchased the BSA C10L back in 2000 when I moved back to Yorkshire. The start and finish was at RAF Wickenby, a former Lancaster bomber station and from where many brave young men failed to return. Being in Lincolnshire meant it was ideal country for old machines (and riders), but for me the real challenge was making the round trip of 120 miles to reach the start, then adding a further 50 miles of by-ways through the old County of Lindsey.

While there may have been a dearth of pre-1931 events in my immediate area, by being a member of the Yorkshire Vintage Motorcyclists provided enough outings, including some nation wide publicity on a BBC programme featuring Yorkshireman, Alan Titchmarsh. The programme was entitled 'The Village Show' and was one in a series depicting typical events and displays of English village life. Several members brought along machines on the assumption that there would be space amongst the prize marrows and giant pumpkins to show our vintage treasures. However, when the programme came to be transmitted, the producer must have decided that we did not depict English village life and we finished up on the cutting room floor! All was not lost though, for we received better coverage in Old Bike Mart after Secretary, Keith Bastow, sent a group photograph and a brief history of the Club.

Before we leave the 'Naughties', that dreadful euphemism given to the first nine years of the new century, it may be poignant to catch up on what had been happening with the other 'stable occupants. The B44 was still rattling away nicely. "They all do that sir." I did tend to use this more for long country runs away from urban centres, as I began to notice that my approach always caused heads to turn, curious at the sound. Even dogs on leads would look round, while grazing cattle and horses always raised their heads to check out the sound in case it was the farmer on his tractor with more fodder! As for me, what I heard inside my crash helmet did not sound too much out of the ordinary for an ageing British single cylinder motorcycle.

The BSA M20 was also contributing to the annual mileage by now showing a total of over 8500. Section runs in East Yorkshire were the main outings, but the long established Topcliffe Rally organised by the North East Section was a regular annual run. Their route always varied from lush green pastures to the bleakness of the North Yorkshire Moors. Also, I could never resist the challenge of me and the M20 against Sutton Bank. To date I've always been on the winning side! One run on the M20 involved a lunch stop at Cadwell Park and we were allowed 2 laps around the circuit. Despite seeing 56 MPH on the speedometer, I just could not get the front wheel in the air on the Mountain section! Having previously hinted at my inherited habit of logging mileages, perhaps I should come clean and own up to it being more of an obsession, as I detailed each journey in miles, fuel purchased, repairs carried out and parts replaced. Each riding season is rounded off with an average MPG check. If you think it sounds boring, just make sure you don't sit next to me on a non-corridor train! To round off this period, in 2008 I completed the longest journey in a day and never bettered since. 260 miles in fact to see my old pal, Arthur, in Leicestershire. He was a lovely character who began working for Rudge Whitworth in Coventry at the age of 12 in 1932. He learnt to ride a motorcycle during the first few weeks through a tunnel which ran under the street between the two factories. During the Coventry blitz he had ridden an M20 while serving as an ambulance driver and his last outing on 2-wheels was in 2010 on his 90th birthday.

Then of course there was the BMW R65, still the youngest machine in my collection and, at the time of writing, I have never owned a motorcycle later than 1982. At the start of 2008 with the mileage showing 50,000, I carried out a major service from fork seals to carburettor needles and jets. It now became my long distance choice, not necessarily in VMCC events, but whenever I wanted a decent ride out and by decent, that usually meant 150 or more miles. It was about this time that I began to search back into the family history. There had always been a mystery about one of Dad's uncles who died in the first week of the Battle of the Somme in 1916. Joe Mellor had been the brother of Grandfather Mellor and at the outbreak of war had, like so many other young men, volunteered to join the local City force as part of the West Riding Regiment known as the Leeds Pals. During the opening week of the Somme campaign the 'Leeds Pals' were decimated, there being few survivors to return to their home City and Joe was one of thousands who were never found and had no known grave.

What scant information the family had on his death was written on the back of one of the last photographs taken before he left England, and this was no more than a name which may have referred to a field or an area where a skirmish had taken place. My research discovered that they had trained on the moors above Masham in North Yorkshire, moving to barracks at Ripon before being posted abroad. Once I had amassed all this information, I set off on the R65, first to find the site of the training camp high on Colsterdale Moor. To my emotional joy, I found there were not only still visible traces of the camp but a memorial in the form of an obelisk with an inscription to the regiment and their sacrifice.

While taking photographs a Land Rover, with the obligatory sheepdog looking out of the window, stopped and the farmer asked if I had a family connection to the site. He then went on to tell me more details of the area, and that his father had been involved in some of the construction work. The conversation then turned to motorcycles and he asked if I attended the memorial service each November on Remembrance Sunday. What followed was of even greater interest as he told me about a group of motorcyclists that came every year, one of them bringing a portable radio to hear the 11am service from the Cenotaph in London and observing the 2 minutes silence.

I attended for the first time in November, 2008 when around 20 motorcyclists gathered, including a few familiar faces from VMCC events. Since then it has become my traditional final outing of the year on the R65 and numbers have steadily grown. One of the last surviving colonels of the West Riding Regiment also attends with his family and always pays grateful thanks to all who have ventured out on what can be a difficult time of the year with regard to weather conditions. Happily, to date the weather has always been favourable for the sombre occasion. If it does happen to fall on the 11th of November, being Dad's Birthday, is also very poignant.

Before we enter the period of the tens and teens, (no, I don't like the term either.) there is one more machine to introduce to you. I'll bet it's a BSA I can hear you chorusing. Well, you are right, but with a twist. You are going to learn about a Basuki! Never heard of one? Then read on. One of the many people I met in our wonderful world of motorcycling was the late, Alan Clarke. Originally from Leeds, I first met him and his brother Len, back in 1994 while taking part in the end to end trip and when I moved back to Yorkshire, it was pleasing to find he had moved to North Yorkshire too and was often present on section runs. Alan lived a humorous life as I found out during the journey from Groats to Land's End. He and Len certainly enriched the evenings at each overnight stop.

Alan was now living in a charming village near Ripon and for a number of years, his cottage was the start of some enjoyable tours, organised in aid of the Yorkshire Air Ambulance. It was pleasant countryside whichever direction you went. West to Wharfedale, east to the Hambleton Hills or north to Scott Trial country in Swaledale. He had some interesting machines, including a Triumph Thunderbird with matching sidecar in which his wife, Barbara, would navigate. Another machine and the one that first caught my interest was based around a Francis- Barnett. This had been fitted with a 250cc Honda engine with an electric starter and I could immediately see the potential of such a machine as the years advanced. The time when knee joints began to lose that action so quaintly described in owners handbooks as, 'a long swinging kick.'

I hatched a plan around a basic British 250cc single, which narrowed the choice to one of the final products to come out of BSA, as the shadows began to lengthen on the Small Heath Company. The B25 was an ideal model. The cycle parts were tried and tested, it boasted a twin-leading shoe front brake and the frame offered ample room for a larger capacity battery to handle the electric starting. Another plus factor came when Jim Lee informed me he had purchased an MOT failure for spares to support the Susuki GN250 he already owned. Thus was the seed sown.

Having acquired the Susuki engine along with all ignition electrics, I began searching for a suitable BSA B25, eventually buying a 1970 American import, which had already been issued with a BSA Owners Club dating certificate. This indicated that it left the BSA works in January, 1970 destined for Baltimore and proved invaluable when applying for an age related number. It was pleasing to find that my local DVLA Office at Beverley issued a redundant Hull number. There began a long period of measuring, photographing and making templates to compare with the BSA B25 dimensions. It appeared to work and of course I could take many measurements from my B44, being an almost identical frame. The only doubt concerned the brake pedal which would need re-positioning to the right hand side. As Sherlock Holmes used to say, "It was a three pipe problem."

It was not helped by the BSA brake drum being on the left hand side, leaving only two alternatives. Either a crossover shaft for the pedal or a cable operated brake. But this raised another problem. The smallest sprocket that would fit the brake drum was 46 teeth, which gave a top gear ratio far too low for serious road use. Once again, I went down that John Logie Baird route, first making a cable operated brake and fitting the smallest sprocket available. The first road test was disappointing to say the least. Even with a 5-speed gearbox and the largest gearbox sprocket that could be accommodated, the available top speed was unsuitable. As for the cable operated rear brake, it certainly would not have registered a pass on the MOT tester's meter. So it was back to the drawing board and plan 'B'.

The problem was solved by fitting the rear wheel from a Susuki GN250 model. Although this meant fitting the BSA 18" rim in place of the original 16" to retain the BSA appearance and ground clearance. Now with the correct gearing the whole performance was transformed, turning the B25 into a most delightful machine, be it on a long distance journey or merely covering the green lanes over the Yorkshire Wolds. If only Small Heath had produced such a machine 45 years ago, how different British motorcycle history could have been. With it's 4-valve engine and twin swirl combustion chamber, it does everything that an ageing motorcyclist requires, it has also become a good conversation opener wherever I stop. And I know Dad would have been intrigued.

Early in 2009 that doyen of the vintage motorcycle world, Noel Whittall, from Leeds, came up with an idea to establish an annual event that could be a northern alternative to the Banbury Run. The proposed title was, 'The Golden Era Run' and from that time it has become established as a first class event. The start and finish was to be at Elvington Air Museum, near York and was to include a lunch for all riders after completion of a course that took in easy going countryside, ideally suited to early veteran machines. I entered the York and being only 20 miles distant, it was an easy ride to the start. The day was a pleasant one, even though I was bombarded with questions as to whether the York was built in York? I again entered the event in 2010 and this time I prepared myself for interrogation by printing some simple pamphlets giving a potted history for those who enquired.

2010 also saw me back at the Banbury Run, now established at the Heritage Centre at Gaydon in Warwickshire. This time I heeded my own advice that I could do better, and I did. My total time was close enough to qualify for a Silver Medal and in so doing, I flew up Sun Rising Hill in second gear with no obstructions. It was a good feeling even if the York was a very basic and cheaply built machine. While it lacked the elegance of the Sunbeam and the panache of the CS 1 Norton and did not have the military bearing of the Triumph model H, in it's crude and simple form, the York was no different from dozens of other manufacturers products of the period that were supplying a demand. Sadly few of them survived to the end of the 'hungry' thirties. It did the job it was built for. Dad often said that machines of the late twenties were little different from those of ten years later, save possibly for the introduction of the the foot gear change. Also by the late twenties, reliability had become the norm, to such an extent that it passed unmentioned. As Canon Basil Davies, better known as 'Ixion',(which he insisted should be pronounced, 'Icks-eye-on,') stated, "If I take the train to Edinburgh, I do not report to my hosts that the engine achieved 80MPH near Grantham, or that it covered the 400 miles without a breakdown."

In the case of my machines I suppose they had become reliable, even predictable. As for technology the BMW R65 had more electronic circuits than the British machines. In the case of the York the electrics consisted of a battery, three bulbs and a dip switch. The B44 had the sophistication of electronic ignition, while the M20 supported the good old mag/dyno, a well tried and tested piece of equipment as I could vouch for from my apprentice days as an auto-electrician. So often did I find a unit that was being stripped for overhaul still showing a healthy spark. The two little 'C' models both supported coil ignition, that much maligned system on many early cheap motorcycles. I have lost count of how many times a motorcyclist has told me about it being unreliable and battery dependant. My answer was to ask them how many cars they had owned that were fitted with a magneto?

Also in 2010 Titch Allen's Relay Rally was back again. Once again I began by signing on at my local East Yorkshire checkpoint, then by using the Humber Bridge, another first for me on a motorcycle, I rode to the Mid Lincs. Section point. While crossing the Humber Bridge, I reminded myself that 28 years earlier, I had been there for the opening ceremony as part of an ITN News Crew. The result of my sound is still available to hear on Google by typing, 'Humber Bridge Opening, 1982. Make of it what you will, but my only claim to fame is that there are few people in Britain who have not heard my work, be it drama, documentary or news and current affairs.

Out of the blue I was contacted by the Editor of the now defunct magazine, Off Road Review. This took a monthly look back at all varieties of motorcycle sport, including grass track racing and included regular features by such illustrious names as, Ralph Venables, Don Morley, Jim Reynolds and Mike Jackson. The suggestion was that I write a series of articles on Yorkshire Grass Track racing, which in it's parochial way, differed from the events held in other parts of Britain for the retention of rigid frames and girder forks, plus the fact that tracks were usually no longer than 400 yards. As opposed to those in the south of England, where 1200 yards was commonplace, along with rear suspension, telescopic forks and four speed gearboxes.

The articles proved popular and I was contacted by a few former riders who added some of their own recollections. Further research soon established that from a regular entry list dating back to the beginning of the 1950s, there were now fewer than 20 survivors. It was a sobering fact. With all the gathered information, plus photographs sent by family members of former riders, I decided to publish a reminder of this period of unique motorcycle sport, based around the meetings held at agricultural shows in the Yorkshire Dales when the word sponsorship was in no ones vocabulary and you could buy a set of leathers in any colour, so long as it was black!

Using the title, 'Dales Tales', I tried to convey in words and pictures some of the atmosphere of the period, along with the delightful characters who came to the starting lines in this still austere period after world war two. The first print run sold out quickly and the reprint has dwindled to just a few remaining copies. I now find it very rewarding to see the book being offered on eBay at a price in excess of what I charged. I say rewarding because my intention had been to leave a memento to those stalwarts who remained faithful to a primitive style of grass track machine, devoid of any frills or refinements. Little wonder we were known as the 'flat earth grassers'! One of these was Dick Wilkinson, father of Trials ace, Bill Wilkinson, from Kettlewell in Wharfedale. I wanted to pass on a copy to Bill so made it part of a route along Wharfedale and Wensleydale. As I passed through Kilnsey, I stopped to look across to the field, where 60 years earlier Dick Wilkinson and I had been entered for the grass track races that followed Kilnsey Show. When I left Bill's garage, I could not resist pitting the BMW against the still tortuous climb up Park Rash.

As 2010 drew to a close, I felt satisfied that all machines had contributed to my motorcycling pleasure. The York had now totted up 4000 miles and I was already being dubbed as the 'Yorkie Bar Kid! The M20 had also given good service, including the annual climb of Sutton Bank. But the serious mileage was again down to the BMW, totalling 1575. This made a collective total of 5007 using 6 machines, as I had declared SORN for the

BSA B44 with a view to try and reduce some of the rattles. I was also looking at the possibility of reducing the compression ratio from the standard 9 to 1 as it was becoming harder to produce that 'long swinging kick.' Time never seemed to be on my side. With 7 motorcycles to maintain, even though some of the annual mileages were small, it was often the case of what you thought would be an hour's job turning into something more complicated. Added to this I had inherited over 1000 master recording tapes of music that I and sound colleague, Les Brumpton, had recorded over a 40 year period. As I had always maintained a record company label name for small productions, it now seemed an appropriate time to enlarge this and make the material available to a wider audience. The fact that 6 years later it is still in existence, despite the continuing demise of the compact disc, does indicate an appreciative audience.

A large part of 2011 was devoted to machine maintenance as tyre wear, along with chains, brake linings and electrical components all seemed to coincide for replacement. All of this had to be fitted into a working day running the record company and expanding my research of the family tree, particularly regarding information on Uncle Joe. Since making contact with several military historians following my annual trips to the Leeds Pals Remembrance Service each November, I had amassed a wealth of information. Who said being retired was dull? No union would have stood for the amount of hours I was devoting to each pursuit. The down side was of course my annual mileage suffered and by the end of the year I could only log 1100 miles. Once again my Headmaster's comment came to mind. I was determined to improve on this during 2012 with particular emphasis on the York. Since I had told old Arthur Grant down in Leicestershire it's history, he had said on a number of occasions that he would like to see the machine and as he knew where the old factory was in Croft Road, Coventry, I began planning a country route to avoid the main centres of traffic.

Once I had devised a suitable route, I then calculated what the fuel consumption would be. My intention being to carry enough spare fuel to cover the whole trip, thus saving the need to search for petrol stations. By using plastic containers I could dispose of these in lay-by litter bins, lightening my load as I went along. It became one of the most enjoyable trips I have ever undertaken. A round trip of 250 miles, an 83 year old machine in the hands of a 78 year old rider. It gave me a near perfect insight to what motorcycling in the 1920s was like. When I arrived at Arthur's home, only 3 miles from Kirkby Mallory, he was overjoyed. Not only had a young whipper snapper like me ridden a hand change machine such a distance and bear in mind I was 14 years his junior, he then went into a long explanation of the pros and cons of the JAP engine when compared to a Rudge. When it came to motorcycles, he had seen them all and coming from Coventry he was in a good position to judge. Arthur was one of those people I have already mentioned, able to do everything to keep a motorcycle on the road and after leaving the Rudge Company, he served his time with Alfred Herbert Engineering. His skills were put to good use after the war as I'm sure many elderly motorcyclists in and around Coventry may remember. Before leaving the year, it is perhaps appropriate to mention my trip to the Somme Battlefields. This fulfilled all the time and research I had spent on Uncle Joe Mellor when I found his name listed, along with 72 thousand others with no known grave, on the memorial at Thiepval in Picardy.

My annual mileage had risen, but there was room for improvement and it was all going to happen in 2013. The plan was to use one machine with the sole purpose of mileage building and it was going to be the Basuki with which I had now found a preference for. The ease of starting on a cold morning, plus all the appearance of a good old British single brought a lot of simplicity to my motorcycling and by adding indicators, meant I could extend my riding season into late November. Trying to give hand signals in the half light of an autumn afternoon can be fraught with danger. It was a simple plan. Whenever I went out I was determined to add at least 100 miles for each trip, but of course many were considerably more. One of them was another trip to show the Basuki to Arthur Grant. Simply because the last machine he rode in his nineties was a Susuki GN250. It was such a joy to ride, and I speak from years of riding rigid frame machines, that it became my choice for many section runs in addition to solo tours. It was also pressed into service for my annual Remembrance Sunday trip to Colsterdale, due to the BMW R65 only for the third time in 10 years and 58 thousand miles letting me down. Only ten miles from home too, when I lost all drive due to the clutch plate centre becoming lose. Even the little C11 added 500 miles to the annual tally, but it was the Basuki with a total of 3750 miles that took the running total to my all time record of a whisker short of 7000 miles. When I mentioned to

'Dick' Lewis, the BSA Guru of many years standing, that around half the mileage had been achieved on BSA machines, he teasingly said, "Not bad for a young 'un." Will I try and break it? I do still have some ambitions left which is perhaps why I had chosen to break the mileage record while still in my seventies, perhaps hedging my bets, for within four months and into 2014, the 'eight zero arrived.

A peculiar trait of British people when finding the age of someone has reached 80, is to ask how it feels to be 80. This is then usually followed with, "Well, you don't look 80." Anyone who has already passed such an age, will understand the slight irritation. How are you supposed to feel. You have had no experience of being that age and as for not looking your age, my answer is usually something like, "You should be in my shoes!" The great problem with growing old is, while the joints, sinews and bones show signs of weariness, the mind remains young and active, giving a belief that you can do all the things you have always undertaken. Only when you come to try and do them do the problems begin. So for those fellow motorcyclists who have yet to become octogenarians, permit me to pass on the following. Just carry on as normal. If everything was working fine the day before why should anything change.

March, 2014 did not get off to a good start but as the end of the month neared the weather improved and the BMW was prepared. Although not aware at the time, it was in fact 21 years to the week since buying it so an anniversary run was in order. I had of course already planned a birthday celebratory ride which was due in another 3 weeks. You may ask why did it seem so important? Many people reach the age of 80. I can only give you my reasons. Looking back over the years many dear friends and colleagues did not make that age,some of them did not even see the new century and as 64 of the years had provided me with a wealth of pleasure, friendship and achievement on 2-wheels, why not make it a celebration. After all, it was only continuing a family quirk.

When the birthday week arrived spring was truly in the air with near perfect motorcycling conditions. Too good to miss in fact. On the day in question I took the BMW on one of my devised circular routes which I had christened the 'bridges' route. This took in the River Trent crossing at Keadby, then over the Humber Bridge and finally Boothferry Bridge over the River Ouse. The next day I was out on the 250cc BSA C11 on one of my local villages route and I rounded off the week with a Pre-1931 event with my local East Yorkshire Section, adding a further 107 miles to the York. When May came it was time for the bi-annual VMCC Relay Rally and upon seeing that one of the Lakeland Section signing on points was to be manned by Stan and Grace Harper, my choice of machine just had to be the BSA B44 Victor, still in the same livery as when I collected it from his house 23 years earlier.

My intention was to try and sign on at a number of other points around the Lakeland area, as that section were hosting no fewer than ten. But as always happens when motorcyclists start talking, time slips by. Aided by the fact that Stan and Grace were in their well stocked camper van and once the kettle was on and the sandwiches kept coming, before I knew it four hours had passed and it was time to return south. The round trip added 220 miles making a total close to 21 thousand in 23 years, all of which had been free of major troubles. The whole journey had been a delight and I began to rue that I had neglected the old thumper for so long. Having electric starting on a motorcycle is very convenient, but it perhaps introduces you to complacency which can easily turn you away from a big single with a high compression. On the journey home I vowed to take action and reduce it by means of fitting a compression plate and although it may soften the performance, at my age do I need to worry. Sadly, like all our best plans the job is still unfinished. However, one day!

I rounded off 2014 by visiting several of my country seats. Let me hasten to add these are not ancestral homes, but merely conveniently placed seats which local parishes often place in a picturesque setting around their village. They have become little havens where the goings on in far off places seem of little consequence and as I always take a flask with me, the catering is to my liking. Often I will be joined by another motorcyclist or cyclists and hikers and we often put the world in order by making all the big decisions. We leave the little ones to the Government of the day, such as which trouble spots do we send troops and tanks to, or how many nuclear submarines should we build. My mileage for the year was logged as 4650.

Now I was a fully paid up member of the octogenarian club there are a number of points worth mentioning. First there is a noticeable change in the attitude of young people. Ken Dodd summed it up when referring to young people this way, "You find teenagers eager to help you onto the bus, even when you've just got off the blasted thing!" Maybe we are viewed with a sympathetic nature because we are no longer a threat in any way to their welfare or activities. I recall that during my last working years, a young assistant would feel uneasy when needing to ask my advice about a certain task, whereas with someone nearer to his age group he could behave with complete assurance. Maybe it's a 'male thing', because I find girls do not suffer the same inhibition. On a recent visit to London and a tube journey on a line that I was not familiar with, brought help immediately from girls who must have sensed my unease with trying to work out where I needed to change. Two girls even offered me their seats.

We are now coming to the penultimate year before the actual centenary. Is it going to be a time of reflections and reminiscences? Not just yet for I feel the appropriate time would be once the final year is with us, only then can I begin to look back upon past times. I just have to make sure I get there first. For the present there was another season of motorcycling to be completed, although I was becoming a little bit more selective with the weather, rather than my previous attitude of taking a chance. Modern motorcycling clothing is now streets ahead of what I started out wearing and even assuming it keeps out the rain, there is no real enjoyment, certainly not when wearing an open face helmet with just a visor. Being the old fashioned type I have never taken to the modern full face helmet mainly because on the occasion I tried one, I found the side vision somewhat restricted, particularly when taking a rearwards glance to cover any blind spots in the mirror's view.

I started out with a plan for 2015. First and foremost was to devote more time to completing the manuscript for this book and make most of the photograph selections. But once again there were events which none of us can predict. In the first three months I lost three friends, two of whom were work colleagues, the third being dear old Arthur Grant who died four days short of his 95th birthday. Then there were new record projects to complete, two of which involved location recordings. The old joke about the retired pensioner being so busy, he was thinking of setting a lad on, never rang truer. Easter Monday was early this year which is always a good excuse for getting a few miles in, although I had already put 250 miles on Basuki during March.

By the time the first section road events were beginning, all machines had been running, with the exception of the BSA B44. I had in fact actually made a start to remove the engine from the frame, but I am ashamed to admit that the compression plate has yet to be fitted. One loss that occurred on the first day of May was the death of one of Britain's finest racing motorcyclists. Geoff Duke was a name that became synonymous with the T.T races and of course Norton, the machine that took him to his first World Championship. It was while Editor of the Association of Pioneer Motorcyclists Newsletter that I first came into contact with him, when he became a member. But it was through his company that specialised in motorcycle videos and sound recordings that regular contact was established when I was able to put him in touch with someone who had rare film and tape recordings of the T.T.races. His appearance at the 70th Anniversary Dinner of the Association was an occasion to remember and I have always regreted not recording his reminiscences, along with Phil Heath, Ivan Rhodes and Arthur Wheeler. I remember telling him, that as a youngster I had been in the Island for his first Clubman's win, also his first T.T. win. His only comment was, "Did it look fast?"

By the time midsummer arrived, It was becoming apparent that it was not going to be a high mileage year. First the weather did not make an ideal summer with August producing a higher than average rainfall, then there were two more funerals to attend. Each one then led to a reunion of old colleagues, all vowing to stay in touch and declaring that we should do it more often. Isn't there an old saying about the road to Rome being paved with good intent. Maybe it's not Rome, but it sounds better, however, fitting it all into the normal day when you have so many interests, to say nothing of the everyday domestic needs is never going to be easy. To make up my mileage I was now taking every opportunity to hit the highway or more appropriately, the country lane. Many of the outings amounted to no more than 50 miles but as they say north of the border, "Many a Mickle macks a Muckle." No I haven't a clue what it means either!

A couple of journeys brought the M20 into use and once again after the first few miles, I was rueful of neglecting the old side valve for so long. It was a machine conceived in the 1930s just as I was and we seemed to go together so well. However, the routes I took were easy gradients with little chance to produce that characteristic BSA 'slog.' As high summer arrived it seemed that all the conflicts within the Vintage Motorcycle Club had receded, at least to a point where most members had accepted that despite all the pitfalls of the previous year, a steadier hand was now in control. What direction the Club was heading for was still not certain as Section Organisers battled with the problem of fewer and fewer vintage machines compared with later models bearing yellow number plates, all of course qualifying under the rolling 25 year rule. It was a case of never being able to please everyone. Some even suggested a change of name to incorporate the word 'Classic.'

What had to be accepted by many senior members was a simple fact that anyone born after say, 1960, would have little or no knowledge of British motorcycles. I came across such an example during my working days when I befriended a young man who later went on to be a 'high flyer' in the legal profession. At 17 his parents had bought him a 125cc Honda for transport to and from college and it gave him so much pleasure and satisfaction, it was replaced by a larger model which served him well for the next five or so years, including a touring holiday of Britain. As his fortieth birthday coincided with the dawn of the new century, he was about to buy his fifth Honda twin and it was around this time that I introduced him to Tragatsch's Encyclopedia of Motorcycles, illustrating that a number of Japanese twins were copies of earlier British models.

He became so enthralled in the discovery of a once flourishing industry he took out a subscription to Old Bike Mart and following a visit to see the start of the Banbury Run, he became fascinated with machines of the twenties. The final initiation came when he read an advertisement for a 1926 Sunbeam which was described as 'a gentleman's motorcycle' and felt this would be his type of machine. The immediate outcome was a happy one and he enjoyed six summers of vintage motorcycling along the lanes of Berkshire. Sadly, before reaching his fiftieth birthday he had already been diagnosed with some strange illness and didn't reach his half century.

So how do you attract young people to join a club that has a high percentage of pensioners as members? My own personal opinion is, I don't think you can. From being a teenager I recall that my interests only gave a cursory glance to anything that had a belt drive and flat tank. I also remember that out of a crowd of fellow school leavers all hell-bent on making their mark in some form of motorcycle competition, only two did. Just for the record, we are still in touch despite the fact that David now lives 4000 miles away in Canada. As for the remainder, all were driving cars by the time they received the 'key of the door.' So it would seem to be down to just two factors. Either you inherit your love of motorcycles or you have that free spirit that seeks out enthusiasm and camaraderie. Away perhaps from the restraints of the workplace that may be tedious, seeking a world apart from the Monday to Friday routine. The motorcycle can provide all this, no matter what your personal status may be or your mechanical skills. It is a common bond to all those who love riding, or to use that lovely old English word, just 'fettling' motorcycles.

Now autumn had arrived. That season so beloved by landscape artists with leaf strewn scenes of countryside and lanes. For the motorcyclist this can be a time of great danger as wet and slimy leaves are as perilous as loose gravel or even ice. I wonder if the modern motorcyclist heeds those old words of 'Carbon', in his weekly column in Motor Cycling about reducing your tyre pressures by a couple of pounds as a precaution. Perhaps the modern tyre with all the research of sticky substances, carbon fibre re-enforced walls and heat controlled surfaces are immune to such hazards. Nevertheless, it is a time for alertness and careful brake applications.

With the start of November, forecasters were warning of wet weather for much of the month. They followed this with a light hearted explanation that it was all down to the 'jet stream' 200 miles above the earth, which was little comfort for those of us who were trying to dry out the 'Barbour', Bellstaff, Weise or Frank Thomas. It was so intense I had to miss my annual ride on Remembrance Sunday to the 'Leeds Pals Memorial', high on the moors above Masham, my first miss in eight years. Once again it was a case of not wanting to start out in pouring rain, but if it happens en route that is just part of motorcycling.

By the time December arrived and all hope of one more dry and mild day fading, it was time for some serious planning of which maintenance jobs had to be tackled first. With now under 30 days before the start of 2016 I had at last begun to remove the tank, carburettor and exhaust pipe on the B44 Victor in preparation for fitting a compression plate. On the larger BSA unit engine, it is necessary to remove it from the frame, due to insufficient height to clear the top tube when removing the cylinder head. There is a quick method, although never recommended by the factory. This entails removing the rocker studs and sliding it to one side, enabling the head to be lifted. Were it an iron cylinder head I suppose you could get away with it. But steel studs into alloy threads can suffer from repeated removal.

The York had a number of jobs that had kept being put back to the bottom of the list. The Pilgrim oil pump was becoming difficult to regulate and was also allowing oil from the tank to flow past into the crankcase. There were a number of threads around the engine and gearbox that needed attention. Again it was a case of 80 plus years of being screwed in and out that can do the damage, especially with the fine cycle thread. Helicoil is one solution, but I tend to favour the 'Radco' method which uses the coarse Metric thread and although slightly larger, does not look out of place to the average eye. For those with an above average eye, turning the shank back to Imperial size would satisfy those who criticise such things. On the BMW there were a number of cosmetic jobs to attend to which kept falling into the category of, 'I'll get around to it one day.' That day was now rapidly approaching as was the centenary year of family motorcycling.

As I listened to the church bells ringing in the New Year, now accompanied by the obligatory barrage of fireworks, my thoughts were turning to how I would sum up my contribution to the centennial year of family motorcycling. I could begin by trying to analyse what type of motorcyclist I was. Cautious? Probably. Assumptive? Never, based on the teachings of Dad that you should never assume anything regarding other road users and he was basing his theory on traffic numbers of the 1920s. At the end of December 2014 there were 35.6 million vehicles licensed for use on our roads. Having priority at roundabouts is just one of many examples I could cite where the vulnerability of a motorcycle is greatest. Giving way to traffic from the Right can never be taken as an assumption even when the approaching motorcyclist has a flashing indicator. Hand signals can have a more awakening effect for those drivers enclosed within a reverie of nicotine and recycled hot air aided by 50 Watts of Mega-bass. Even then caution has to be the watchword with a hand or foot poised ready for an emergency brake application.

So all though I will never enter the 'Speedsters' hall of fame I can answer any cynicism for my wariness by stating "I live longer that way." I could also add that I have never fallen off a motorcycle. On grass track and speedway yes, but not while riding on the road. Way back in 1950 when taking my motorcycle test, the first words of the Examiner still linger in my memory when he said, "I want you to remember the three C's. care, consideration and courtesy." I wonder if any of those words are mentioned during todays driving lessons or even when taking the test. So to sum up my years as a motorcyclist, may I add one final statistic that many colleagues find staggeringly hard to believe. The fact that I have never travelled faster than 65 mph on two wheels. Due largely to never having owned anything capable of achieving such a speed, also in latter years I have tended to treat engines as I would an animal. I hate to see them being subjected to suffering.

So as I leave the motorcyclists confessional without needing penance I can face 2016 with no feeling of guilt. We are what we are and life will go on no matter what. If I still have any ambitions left they are now no more than far away dreams. It would have been nice to complete another 'end to end' journey, but with a variation from the traditional route. Something like from Durness in the north west of Scotland to Dungeness in Kent. At a guess the distances are probably similar. Also I had a notion of a trip to the west of Ireland, the Ring of Kerry possibly and if I could accomplish the journey on a pre-1931 machine that would round off the story nicely. But as I write this in the dark days of January, 2016, it is no more than a day dream.

As the daylight hours began to extend, I was encouraged to do some forward planning of which jobs to take on first. I have never been one to tackle more than one job at a time and the thought of having several repair jobs awaiting completion can only lead to disaster. My RAF training had at least served me well so far as methodical servicing was concerned. As my old Flight Sergeant often reminded us, "What we try and aim at is the same number of landings as take offs!" I was already thinking about my local section's first outing towards the end of March and had in mind to use the BSA 'Basuki', it being the the easy option with just general preparation work needed. The fact that it was nearest the garage door played a part also. All it required was to check the tyre pressures, lubricate the rear chain and because it was the first run of the new season, check the sparking plug. As it happened, this proved unnecessary as it's condition was just the way authors of maintenance manuals down the years have described, "A brown, tan or grey appearance is indicative of correct engine running conditions." Don't ask me how guv, I just put petrol in it and ride the thing!

But at the last minute I had to put plan 'B' into operation for at the first attempt to start the engine, the battery had failed to hold charge over the winter. It was eight years old and I suppose in this age of a 'throw away' culture attitude, it had served me well. So it was a hasty change of plan to the BMW R65 and a quick service check of tyres and oil level. After standing since November, 2015 it only took four or five turns of the engine to fire up after allowing enough time for fuel to fill both carburettors.

As I headed for the section starting point along the road towards Beverley, my first thoughts were I had finally made the century of family motorcycling, something that I had begun to muse about around my 75th birthday. I passed close to Junction 36 of the M62 Motorway with a good view of the three lanes of traffic, ranging from speeding 4 x 4s, zippy 3-door hatchbacks, long distance lorries with a carrying capacity of 44 tonnes and motorcycles easily capable of 100mph. When Dad first started out on his Minerva in 1916 there were more horses on the road than powered traffic and there was no such word as Motorway. As I continued along the A614 I passed quickly across Boothferry Bridge which he'd have remembered when it was a ferry! The nearby Ferryboat Inn is one clue, as is Ferry Lane. For a solo motorcycle the charge was one shilling (5p). If you had a sidecar it was double. And you had to make sure you were there before 10.00pm; or you had a long ride via Selby Toll Bridge. Before the 1921 Road Numbering Scheme, the route was simply known as the Hull to Doncaster Road. There were many other reminders to make comparison with life on the roads one hundred years ago. Horse traffic has now gone, so has steam power. Lumbering charabancs are now replaced with elegant coaches featuring air conditioning, hostesses, toilets, in-drive movies and hot drinks.

Roadside features have changed too, now the motorist serves himself with fuel from multi selective powered pumps on a forecourt that dispenses everything from charcoal to cut flowers. In 1916 it would have been a wooden hut and a man, who was probably the local blacksmith, emptying petrol from 2-gallon cans into a funnel to fill your tank. To augment his income, he might also be able to supply you with a local road map and for cyclists, a puncture outfit. Then there were more cyclists than cars, often in club groups which gave rise to roadside halts serving teas and sandwiches. Now it is the motorist that is catered for, sometimes in plastic and chrome settings and other pseudo pretence at elegance where perhaps the cyclist and motorcyclist are not encouraged to stop. To try and make further comparisons I suppose serves no purpose. Starting a conversation with an opening line, "In the old days," means little to someone who is more than half your age, even though they maybe astride a motorcycle. When Dad began riding there was no one able to make such a claim.

For the rest of 2016, my intention is to just ride a motorcycle and bask in my own pleasure of the years that I have contributed to the family century on two wheels. I intend to enjoy each moment, be it on a machine five years older than me, the York, or one 48 years younger, the BMW R65 and of course there are four others to add to the centennial celebrations, including the BSA B44 which is nearing completion of the fitting of a compression plate. So there is plenty of incentive to be active and by chance, the VMCC Nationwide Founders Relay Rally is to be held on May 1st. This year's event coincides with the seventieth anniversary of the founding of the Vintage Motorcycle Club and the rally is held in memory of the founder, 'Titch Allen.' Doubly appropriate as the rally was his idea too. So for no other good reason, I have unofficially declared that the 'century' of family motorcycling is complete after this date.

Yorkie had it's first outing in mid April with a Pre 31 run organised by my local section, East Yorkshire. The river layout in Yorkshire is either North to South or East to West, therefore it is the bridge crossings that govern the route, no matter which direction the journey. In my case it is invariably crossing the River Ouse at Boothferry to reach local section events. The A614 at this point is now a pleasant ride, following the opening of the nearby M62 Motorway with it's lofty crossing of the Ouse a mile downstream. With a 50 mile route over the Wolds I was able to add another 95 miles to the log, bringing the running total to just under 6000 miles. Not bad for an old'un. The York has performed well too!

As the day dawned on my imaginary century I had already scanned the TV channels for local weather reports and it seemed to be a case of perm any one from four. Vague forecasts such as, showers will become lighter or a front is moving in with a chance of a shower were no guide, so it was 'make your mind up' time. My route to the checkpoints was already planned and donned in waterproofs I was on the road by 8.30am with a nice feeling of satisfaction that I had achieved that private ambition to keep riding motorcycles until 2016.

The purpose of the book has been to tell the story of motorcycling by one family over the past 100 years and my hopes are that this has been fulfilled as I reach the final pages. Titch Allen's idea of a Relay Rally to unite members of the Vintage Motorcycle Club is a fitting way to conclude those passing years with some brief notes of my trip on May 1st. 2016. All my intended checkpoints were within Yorkshire so I was literally on home ground covering many roads I had first discovered back in 1950 after passing my driving test. The first checkpoint was at Squires Cafe manned by members of the Wakefield & West Yorkshire section. This is a well known venue throughout Yorkshire catering for the modern 'biker, so the appearance of strange looking motorcycles that were once the pride of a flourishing British industry hardly warrant a second glance.

I then headed north to the North East section's point at Alne and by using one of my country routes, I was able to pass over one of the few remaining private toll bridges in England at Aldwark.

The owner is a former employee of Panther Motorcycles and is perhaps a clue as to why only motorist have to pay a toll. Anyone who arrives on a pre war machine is usually subjected to a barrage of questions about it's history, sometimes to the chagrin of waiting motorists in the queue. I arrived at the home of Jim Wood just as rain began to fall and was soon enjoying refreshments around a wood burning stove with two other members, one from west of the Pennines, the other from Morpeth. Jim is well known in the vintage movement with interests ranging from motorcycles to tractors and steam power.

An hour soon passed and as the rain had stopped, it was time to head south to my final stage at Fimber in East Yorkshire and of course manned by members of that section. Again I took the scenic route which led down a delightful valley carved out of the Yorkshire Wolds mega years ago when our world was still young. I first discovered Thixendale in 1951 on one of my exploratory trips following little known railway branch lines and there have been few changes over the years. Perhaps most significant is the single track road now boasts a splendid Tarmac surface but sadly the cottage that served petrol from a single pump is no more. One thing that has puzzled me down the years about the valley is Ordnance Survey maps give it the name, Waterdale, when in fact there is no trace of water throughout it's length.

The Teapot Cafe at Fimber has become a popular gathering point for the more mature motorcyclist and the banter and fellowship I enjoyed on this particular Mayday, in addition to the novelty of explaining how

I grafted a 250cc Susuki motor into a BSA B25, only went to show what the Vintage Motorcycle Club is all about. With 40 miles to complete the journey home brought the day's total to a satisfying 135miles. This may sound paltry to some members achievements but it was still my special centenary day. However, the story is on-going and there will, hopefully, be many more journeys to enjoy. But now I have to bring an end to the story, taking great care to avoid such hackneyed cliches and phrases that state the obvious. So there will be no suns sinking in the west. No mention of horizons or goals and definitely no doors closing. If I want to end on a philosophical note, I don't need to ask myself what is life? Or who am I? I have probably known the answer all my life. Like my dear old Dad, I'm just the man in the street.